PRAISE FOR *INVOLUNTARY EXIT*

"Empathetic, practical, and empowering guidance for uncertain times. This is more than a book about working through an abrupt career change; it is a book that reminds you of your inherent value, your strengths, and your resources no matter where you're at in life. As Robin beautifully reminds us, you are not alone."

—SARA B. WEEKS, Life Coach

"As Robin demonstrates in this beautiful book, you can move from darkness into the light. The wisdom contained in these pages will assist you on the most important journey of all: happiness."

—BOB COOPER, author of *Heart and Soul in the Boardroom*

"Being savvy about being fired is an essential skillset you never knew you needed. Robin deconstructs the idea of shame and encourages women to reimagine their personal identity and learn how to embrace uncertainty. *Involuntary Exit* is a necessary read for women in the development profession!"

—YOLANDA F. JOHNSON, founder of Women of Color in Fundraising and Philanthropy and president of Women In Development, New York

INVOLUNTARY
EXIT

INVOLUNTARY
EXIT

A Woman's Guide
to Thriving After
Being Fired

ROBIN MERLE

SHE WRITES PRESS

Published 2021
Printed in the United States of America
Print ISBN: 978-1-64742-309-4
E-ISBN: 978-1-64742-310-0
Library of Congress Control Number: 2021910128

For information, address:
She Writes Press
1569 Solano Ave #546
Berkeley, CA 94707

Interior design by Tabitha Lahr

Excerpts from Type R by Ama Marston and Stephanie Marston, copyright © 2018. Reprinted by permission of PublicAffairs, an imprint of Hachette Book Group, Inc.

She Writes Press is a division of SparkPoint Studio, LLC.

For my mother and beloved family,
and all the women who are leaders in their own right.

AUTHOR'S NOTE

This book recounts the authentic experiences of women in the workplace based on interviews and research conducted by the author. In some cases, the names of the individuals and certain identifying circumstances have been changed and composite accounts have been created. This book is intended as a source of helpful advice based solely on the author's views and perspective. It is not meant as a substitute for expert professional advice or for the advice of a competent attorney. Neither the author nor the publisher are responsible for any results or negative consequences resulting from following any advice in this book.

CONTENTS

PREFACE

I wrote this book over two years ago, before the pandemic changed our world and levied a crushing blow to our sense of normalcy. I wrote it before unemployment was at historic highs, with nearly fifteen million people in the US unable to work because their employer closed or lost business due to the pandemic. I listened to women's heartbreaking stories before the advent of Zoom firings, and thousands of people from Weight Watchers were told that they lost their jobs, while they were muted, during a three-minute virtual meeting.[1] Pre-pandemic, when I wrote about professional women being fired, sudden job loss and its traumatic impact was a private phenomenon. We talked about it in huddles with best friends or with people we trusted enough to help us, or we didn't talk about it at all.

COVID-19 changed all that. Stories about unemployed workers filled headlines. About a month after New York City went into lockdown, the *New York Times* introduced an At Home section to help people get through the novelty of a life not circumscribed by work and routine but filled with uncertainty. Uncertainty was the yeast that rose steadily under the heat of the virus. Not knowing what was to come was almost as threatening as the virus itself. Did it make people feel more isolated? Throw them into a rage? Go up and down the seesaw of emotions until they landed at some balance of acceptance and anxiety?

Being thrust into the unknown, without bringing it on yourself, was a broad theme for all of the women interviewed for this book. They lost their jobs, or exited involuntarily at a time of stability in the world, but for them the world was not stable. All of the markers they'd known to define who they were and the purpose they had lived were gone. Their sense of identity, so wrapped up in their positions, became a sense of loss, and at first they struggled to find a way to redefine themselves outside of their jobs. Is this happening now because of COVID-19? Are people questioning their identities and their journeys? How has the pandemic shifted our tolerance for uncertainty?

I asked these questions of Megan Marzo, a licensed clinical social worker with the Weill Cornell Psychiatry Collaborative Care Center, who specializes in cognitive behavioral therapy. She told me that, as a group, the people she is seeing in her practice are more uncomfortable with uncertainty than people have ever been because of how our society has evolved. "If we can't find the answer, we blame ourselves and think something is wrong with us. When we look at the immediate future, it's not clear. We're existing without knowing where we're going to be working or not working—it's destabilizing. Losing a job has people reeling."

These are the feelings that I explored pre-pandemic when the act of being fired was something to be dealt with by entities that now seem quaint, like an outplacement agency or any number of cottage industry specialists that were (1) employed and (2) had little to no training for dealing with the shame and trauma of job loss, no less night sweats about identity and purpose. "Our jobs are the thing we orient our identity around," says Marzo. "There's a newer phenomenon where our job isn't just about gaining resources, it's about who we are, so when we lose that, we feel we're failing at the purpose we decided upon."

The good news is that almost all of the women in this book did step back, reflect, and reinvent themselves after being fired. They did so in their unique ways, which are not so much novel as workable for them. Marzo says she sees a COVID silver lining of people "adapting in beautiful ways. We're hearing people reevaluate priorities as we acknowledge that job loss is often an identity loss. The pandemic has led people to take a step back and question, 'Why is my identity my job? Do I like this? Why am I doing this? Is working hard good?' As behavioral therapists, our goal is to disentangle fact and the story you're telling yourselves about the event. You can challenge your stories and see that a lot of them are changeable and not true."

COVID-19 has taught us many scalding and tragic lessons, but it's also shown us that we have a lot more choices than we could see when we were chugging along day after day. "After the initial shock of trauma and absorption, there is a new forum for growth and opportunity," says Marzo. This is my overarching message to all of you who pick up this book. Whether you've been fired, laid off, been the casualty of a business closure, or simply need to move on, my hope is that you'll emerge with a new set of positive beliefs about your future and your power to change your course however it benefits you. Growth, opportunity, hope. Let's hold on to that.

December 2020

INTRODUCTION: THE DAY THE EARTH STANDS STILL

Your Life Can Change in Thirty Seconds

The day you lose your job will begin like any other day with the whirlwind of a routine that has organized every minute of your life for years. If you are a Type A Loyalist, used to being recognized for all you've accomplished, this break with the reality you've been inhabiting for so long is a stun-gun moment that you'll never forget. Listen to this. . . .

Lindsey had been awake and working since four thirty, sending emails before making her way into the city. By six o'clock, answers were already coming back; this was the usual routine. As soon as she arrived, she was back at it, figuring out the strategies for the day's meetings and what she would focus on to move the needle just one more increment. In her head she carried a top five list of all the multimillion-dollar gifts she needed to close to meet the goals she set for herself. She went to bed with this list and woke up with it, knowing this would drive her every action for this day and every day to come.

She was within minutes of the office when her cell phone vibrated. It was her boss's assistant asking when she would arrive because the boss wanted to see her. "What's the topic?" Lindsey asked. Her organization had just launched a billion-dollar fundraising campaign and had several serious proposals on the horizon—those top five potential gifts in her head. She thought perhaps her boss had good news for her. The assistant simply urged her to see her boss as soon as she arrived.

On her walk over, Lindsey ran through a checklist of all the things he might want to talk about. Did he have a conversation with the new board member about his gift, and did they need to follow up immediately? Should she have told him about her conversation with a major donor who was unhappy about an issue which she had been working to resolve quietly?

Lindsey was what you might call one of those Type A Loyalists. Her job was the most important thing in her life. She was proud of where she worked and what she accomplished and was always "on," dedicated 24-7 to her work family. She had numbers and the ever-increasing goals tattooed on her heart and memory. She had lived this way for three decades, here and elsewhere, loving the chase, loving the success, and pumping up teams until they were as happily driven as she was.

When she walked into her boss's office, he was behind his desk on the phone, and she waited until he motioned for her to come forward and take a seat. He was holding his daily briefing, and she thought she was about to hear that they had received a call from someone who wanted to meet with them that morning to finalize a seven-figure gift. Instead, he looked away, then back to his briefing, and said quickly, "I'm asking you to step down."

Six words . . . less than a minute . . . and her life changed.

There had been no warning from anyone in the organization that she had grown to love over so many years. No heads-up from any of the hundreds of people she worked with up and down the ladder. There was just this sudden announcement on a sunny morning, the two of them sitting in his office where they had sat as partners, carving out strategies together to successfully gain support and build relationships with some of the most influential and powerful people around the world.

Stunned, Lindsey finally found her voice and asked, "Why?" He answered that this was not about her performance. In HR terms—with which she was about to become very familiar—this was not "for cause." It was about taking a new direction.

Lindsey had no contract. Most fundraising executives and staff are "employees at will." In fact, at-will employees make up the majority of the US labor force. When someone later asked her, "Can they just *do* that?" She said, "Yes, they can."

He paused to give her a few seconds before continuing to say words that were completely new to her. For over thirty years, Lindsey had been an A+ star performer who reorganized small fundraising operations into sophisticated businesses. She was numb as her boss described what was about to happen to her, and she asked perfunctory questions, not having any basis or experience to know exactly what she *should* be asking. After all these years, she was stopped in her tracks without any guideposts. Finally, she said the only thing she could think of that bubbled up from a well of respect for herself and for what they had accomplished together: "You have to do whatever you think is right for the organization." He looked at her, surprised, as if expecting a very different response.

That was the last time Lindsey and her boss saw each other or worked together for a common goal. She could not reveal the details of what happened next, just as almost every woman interviewed for this book asked for anonymity for fear of jeopardizing her own or her organization's reputation. I am also a Loyalist, and I can tell you that a separation from a beloved organization, whether wholly or somewhat involuntarily, will have a profound influence on your behavior, sense of identity, and sense of purpose in the days, even years, that follow. If you're stopped cold for the first time in your stellar career, the search for answers will begin the moment you hear the words that change your life.

You may think that Lindsey must have had her head buried in the sand to be so completely surprised. As you'll hear me say many times, knowing the pivotal moment when your fate was decided may always be elusive, and searching backward for answers and clues is not the direction you'll need to be facing the moment you're severed from the company.

I wrote this book because there was no manual for this kind of emotional trauma and recovery, and I was surprised by the depth of shame and disorientation that I and other women experienced. I later learned from Brené Brown's *Dare to Lead* that "shame is one of the most common [emotions] that people feel when they're fired and that the intensity of the shame is related to *how* they're fired." Some bosses use shame as "an outright management tool."[1] The Type A, hardworking, ambitious women I spoke with had stories that they had shared only with their closest other, and advice that was invaluable.

We are more than our jobs and our titles. While this sounds simplistic, women (and men) let positional power determine their identities. When we're in charge, we have people calling us every day, trying to see us, trying to curry favors. We make decisions with authority and confidence that change the direction of organizations. We have staff that we mentor and sponsor and place on career tracks. We make introductions between powerful men and women for the good of the business and, we hope, society. We are leaders. No matter what our titles or positions, we lead. We are programmed to fight upstream and when the water becomes fetid, we become casualties, but that doesn't stop the drive. One fired, energetic leader observed, "They spend two days on orientation at my firm. Why don't they also spend two days on *dis-orientation* when you're let go?"

My hope is that this book will help strengthen your resilience and capacity to respect and build your self-worth. Your emotional upheaval will subside, and you will learn and grow from your experience to discover your unique purpose. The women I interviewed who were suddenly no longer defined by their positional power and who had stepped through the portal of self-discovery are testament to the proof of a positive, self-defined life. As professional coach Bob Cooper says, "We are rarely given the chance, with such clarity and immediacy, to question how we have been spending our hours and how we will manage our lives from this point forward."

I'm not going to tell you it's been easy. On the contrary, I'm going to walk you through the steps and experiences that cause anguish or trigger raw emotions, sometimes when you least expect it, so that you will be prepared to manage your reactions. For example, knowing what you can say legally and what you *want* to say happened is a self-defining process that can take months, even years, of reflection and practice. I will lead you through the emotional arc of your journey, including the unexpected twists, arrhythmic days, anguished public and private moments, and seemingly innocuous triggers that you didn't anticipate. Be assured, those of us who have gone down this road will prepare you so you're not completely blindsided. At least you'll know that when you find yourself, a former manager or executive, spending hours making the smallest decision, that's perfectly okay. Whether you realize it or not, your tiny steps forward are like the white blood cells in your body rushing to help you heal the wounds while you continue to walk around with deep pain. As one woman said after she was let go, "My confidence was in the trash. I didn't feel like I could manage my way out of a paper bag."

These women's stories will help you weigh the pros and cons of sticking around at the company for whatever reason in a demoted position or as a "professional advisor," whether it be for health insurance, retirement benefits, or to keep up the charade that this was a mutually planned succession strategy. "Maybe I'm too literal," said one woman, "but I felt that if I wasn't valued enough in my role, why would I continue to contribute any of my value under a new disguise?"

In researching this book, I've read interesting treatises on "dark leadership," on "bad management," and on corporate culture, and all of these play a role in the stories of women who put their jobs above all else and "drank the Kool-Aid" only to emerge malnourished and hungry for truth and trust. I walk you through how "group think" corporate cultures, employee engagement exercises, and team-building retreats can suppress your sense of control, quash your individualism, and nullify your voice, even if you're a true believer and helped to write the list of corporate values, as many did.

Finally, I take you through what many staff, managers, and leaders put on the back burner or rarely speak about—the spiritual and psychological aspects of what happened to you and why you should start to pay attention to what the universe is telling you. I promise that I won't get too "out there."

I've structured the book to take you through the phases of this journey chronologically. Part One covers the raw emotions of those first hours when a woman is told that she is no longer wanted by her company. You'll hear the stories of how women actually behaved when they heard the news, rather than sanitized versions of these events, so you'll know your reaction is normal. This should be comforting. My goal is to help you negotiate your exit as well as possible so you can retain your dignity. I'll cover the trip to HR, the first telling of what happened, dealing with staff, discussing a severance package, why and when you should talk to a lawyer, the announcement of your departure, and the fear and paranoia that can grow with every revelation about the process. Take heart—squarely facing what happened to you is the first step in healing. Hearing the stories of other women who have not only survived but prospered is also part of the healing process. Knowing that you are not alone, that your feelings are valid, that there is empathy and community behind you is restorative. This is the antidote to withdrawing to a dark corner of your psyche dripping with shame.

In Part Two, we'll explore a phenomenon experienced by many women that I call being "faux-fired." In these scenarios, the organization makes the woman so miserable in her role that she leaves in a huff, essentially firing herself, just as they'd planned. When you hear these stories, you may be stunned by similarities to your own situation and suddenly be able to make sense of comments, actions, and unusual meetings that disconcerted you. This will help you devise a protective strategy or an exit strategy.

Part Three takes you through the real twists and turns of "going public" with your colleagues, friends, and family. You'll learn how to gauge your readiness and state of mind to talk about what happened to you, rather than relying on the standard advice of others outside of your experience. No one but you has your best interests in mind. I'll show you how to be purposeful while treading the waters of uncertainty. We'll learn from other women how they began to reconstruct their personal value while avoiding, but sometimes falling into, the traps of recruiters, networking, and the siren call from the colleagues left behind.

In Part Four, we'll explore how you can begin to embrace uncertainty to open yourself up to completely new opportunities. You'll hear about the techniques successful women used to break old habits and affirm their value. You'll also learn about the emotional triggers that may set you back even when you feel you are ready to move forward. We'll explore the cures for these triggers and help you pump up your fragile new growth. You'll learn about affirmations you will need to practice and believe to change your mindset so you can begin seeing yourself in a new role.

Part Five is your arrival in a "brave new world." You'll hear the stories of women who did the tough work of building resilience and finding their voices again, their special purpose, and their happiness. I'm a realist, so this is not an *aha!* moment but a process that suddenly feels right for you. My hope is that you'll ultimately accept that being fired was a blessing in disguise that has helped you carve out a more rewarding life and a beautiful future.

I interviewed dozens of women for this book and chose to focus on the key stories that had the most to teach us. Unless otherwise indicated, all of their identities and elements of their stories have been disguised. My own story has also been altered. The women I spoke with were between the ages of forty and sixty, some married, some with children, others single. They worked in many industries, ranging from nonprofits to global financial services firms on the East and West Coasts. Almost all the women had achieved a high level of success. Some women had been fired as long as five years ago and still remembered the exact words that shattered their world and their perception of themselves as powerful women. While they are the storytellers, it is also the women coming up in the professional ranks that I hope to reach. Women at greener stages of their careers, who may be tempted by the social seduction of the corporate family, can benefit from these stories' teachable moments and become stewards of their own value as they navigate their way upward.

Finally, while this is written for women, the lessons are applicable to men. I have in fact counseled men who were brave enough to call me to ask for advice or a "heads-up" about what to expect when they were about to be called into their boss's office. Men's stories of being fired are equally harrowing. The fact is that for all of us, when we interlock our identities and value with our positions and job titles, it makes for a very rough landing when it's all taken away.

Consider this your guide to surviving with dignity, self-respect, and excitement for what you can now make happen as the authentic person you are. Throughout the book, I will highlight pieces of advice that I feel are worthy go-tos when you find yourself despairing and in need of perspective. Here is our first one. . . .

BEST ADVICE: The qualities that helped you succeed in your role don't disappear the minute the job does.

Let's get started.

PART ONE

The Loyalists' Guide
to Betrayal

CHAPTER ONE: YOU WERE FIRED. NOW WHAT?

The Disorientation of Exiting

The first twenty-four hours after being fired may be the most difficult of all. There are practical steps to take, emotional waves to manage, and the yearning for privacy and peace while having to perform with a public persona. Often, you must make quick decisions when you don't know whom to trust, what you can say, and how honest you want to be. You are "psychologically dislodged," as one female CEO put it. Therapists call this "cognitive dissonance": when your thoughts and core beliefs don't sync with the reality you're experiencing.

Take comfort in the fact that the dissonance will wane, and your immediate pain and anger will subside as you acclimate to your new way of life. What you won't realize during this upheaval is that this event will reveal so many different strengths and vulnerabilities in you that it's inevitable for you to learn much more about who you are and what you want for yourself and can offer others. You will not immediately see this severance as an opportunity to build strength, but by the end of this journey, you will know that you have been able to survive an intense personal challenge and gain more respect for yourself as a professional. It just doesn't feel good at all in the moment. Listen to these candid memories from powerful women experiencing the first twenty-four hours after they were fired. . . .

"I didn't tell anyone what had just happened to me. I got into bed, fully dressed, and stayed there with my prayer beads."

"I went home and sat in my kitchen. I didn't move for eight hours. I sat in the same clothes in my kitchen for eight hours until my partner came home."

"I drove to an open field, parked my car, and bawled my eyes out. I was lost. I kept asking myself, 'What just happened to me?'"

Why is the disorientation so strong?

You've likely heard of Elisabeth Kubler-Ross's five stages of grief. I prefer a version created by bereavement researchers John Bowlby and Colin Murray Parkes for children who have experienced loss.[1] These stages are more relevant to the bullying that can characterize firings. They include:

1. Shock and Numbness
2. Yearning and Searching
3. Disorientation and Disorganization
4. Reorganization and Resolution

Right now, after the sudden news that you're no longer a part of the firm, there is shock and numbness laced with a searching for answers. The big question is, "Why did this happen to me?"

Based on the stories of the women who were interviewed for this book, performance was not an issue. Regardless, they were told they were no longer wanted. Why?

When it comes to answers, let me get this out of the way: there is always a reason why people are let go. There's the corporate downsizing and job elimination when high salaries are scrutinized. There are the mergers and acquisitions when there can be only one VP of a kind, and the other person is chosen. And of course, there's the new direction, strategic plan, or other business imperative that doesn't include you. Ultimately something wasn't working or in your favor. The kicker is that it was a *secret*. The shocker comes when women aren't *told* it isn't working and have nothing in their file but stellar reviews. Some are even given a promotion and bonus before they're called in and told they no longer have a job.

This is when you look for all the reasons in the world why the company may have taken this course of action. Could it have been your fundamental differences with the CEO about how to grow the business, though you believed you had met him halfway? Was the CEO being pressured by the board to produce more substantial results and taking a calculated risk to preserve his position by bringing in a new team? Was it the meeting where you felt you had won your point but your boss looked like she had just bitten down on a persimmon? Was your compensation too high? Was your age too high? Were you the wrong color? The wrong size? Ultimately, you have to come to terms with the fact that you may never know the exact reason why you were targeted or the precise moment when you became devalued.

The American sociologist Erving Goffman popularized the concept of "front and back stage behavior." "Front stage behavior is what we do when we know that others are watching or aware of us. It's how we behave and interact when we have an audience. Back stage behavior is what we do when no one's looking, or when we *think* no one is looking."[2] Dr. Robert Hogan took this further in his article for the *Harvard Business Review* about the dark side of leadership. He warns us that the dark side comes out of hiding under stress and "often emerges when individuals are dealing with someone they perceive as having lesser status—such as subordinate employees."[3] Imagine staking your value on someone's dark side.

If you are not being fired for "cause," your boss is acting on the front stage, communicating to his audience that he is doing what he feels is necessary for the business. It's the backstage behavior that is undermining. Otherwise, your boss would be taking a different tack—reorganizing or layering, offering 360-degree coaching to help retain loyal senior staff, or rewriting the strategic plan to match current realities. There are any number of ways to course correct before abruptly telling someone it's time to go. We won't be cognizant of the front-stage/backstage behavior when we're in the moment of being told our lives at the company have ended. We're going to be shocked, enraged, cowed, and humiliated.

"I'm fat, fifty, and fired," cried one woman. "I know I don't look like the new people being brought in."

"I wanted to reach across the table and punch him in the heart," said another.

"I told her she should be ashamed of herself and threw the papers on the floor. I wasn't signing anything," said a third.

Some women may break down or let out a fire hose of obscenities the moment the boss delivers the news. Don't, especially if you're in a position to negotiate a separation package. While this may feel cathartic at the time, you want to avoid being escorted out of the building, unleashing your bottled-up anger and frustration to the security guards and staff in the hallways. I guarantee this will be a victory only in your mind or your stories over drinks. It will become company lore, like the story of Marcella who threw her extra suit and raincoat into the recycling bin in her office. Her trashed clothes were found by her coworker. Suddenly stories about Marcella's mental state began to blossom and eventually she became a punch line at company parties . . . not good.

BEST ADVICE: Even under pressure, be strategic. You always have been.

"A woman is like a tea bag. . . . You never know how strong it is until it's in hot water," observed Eleanor Roosevelt.[4] You may feel like a steaming tea bag, but in this moment you want to be as honorable as possible. If this sounds too difficult or abstract, that's perfectly understandable. You'll have plenty of time to think through these moments later when you're no longer standing like the tallest tree in a lightning strike. For now, go mute. Allow yourself to be stunned. There is strength in silence. Your next stop will be Human Resources, where you will want to practice a vow of the monks: the monk shall not speak unless it is necessary.

Humoring yourself can be a survival mechanism, especially in the darkest of moments. If you're able to hold on to your sense of irony, which will be peeking through the curtains of your shock and surprise, particularly as you consider who is staying while you're leaving, it will help you navigate the utter senselessness and land mines of the HR meeting. Don't expect answers from HR. As an executive who has hired and fired, you know how this works. Yet, here you are, on the other side of the table about to become procedure 1128.03. Not for the first time you ask yourself, *Why is it called Human Resources?* instead of its original, more accurate name: personnel management.

BEST ADVICE: Don't confide in the "empathetic" HR person. HR works for the company, not you.

The resources HR provides—like legal protection—are for the company, not you. While HR may present itself as doing the best it can to help you navigate the next steps, HR reports to the C-suite, and HR staff keep their jobs by managing up, not down to you, often becoming the confidante of power. Many women told me that they were "best friends" with the HR person, and in a few cases the HR person was gracious and gently let them know that they'd ship their belongings to them, wanting the on-site process to be over as quickly as possible for everyone's sake. (Human evidence of dark leadership clutters the hallways.) Others said the HR person was waiting outside the door after the firing, and didn't waste a minute before feigning compassion and pressing for the woman's story, so HR could report back to the firing manager on whether or not he was going to have a problem. Still others met with HR people who seemed to enjoy adding to the woman's paranoia of "Why me?" They were adept at giving veiled answers that implied the women were no longer a cultural fit. One of the women who had been fired had been the head of HR herself. She confided that when people asked her why she had been let go, she had to contain herself from repeating the CEO's words that were crude and demeaning. He "wanted something fresh." This wasn't an answer that would make anyone feel better.

The procedural role of the HR person is to make sure your exit is complete. If you have a severance package, they will review it with you to make sure you understand all the terms. They will advise you to have a lawyer read the agreement before you sign it. This, in fact, is the law. As you look at the neatly typed pages that have materialized like a bright white directional arrow showing you to the door, you'll find yourself thinking, *How many people knew about this before I did? How many put this together? When did they know about it? Why didn't any of my "friends" tip me off?*

It's humiliating to think there was a team of people at the company who for weeks, maybe months, knew your fate before you did. They knew about your compensation, your health insurance, your retirement plan, and all the details of your connection with the company. They had spent considerable time calculating what it would cost to part ways. How do you handle this?

Pick yourself up and leave the area. While this may sound simple, it's likely that by this time you're boiling with both fury and insecurity, wanting to hang on to the words being spoken as if hearing more of them will eventually make sense, clear things up, and anchor you to your job. They won't. No matter how many questions you ask, you will not get an answer that makes you feel better. Don't argue or debate. There's no point. The decision about you was made long before this meeting.

You will have time to review the documents later. Many women I spoke with grew silent when asked if they felt they had negotiated well. Others claimed to have gotten a great deal, though admitted there was no way they could know (unless they were in HR themselves or part of a planned layoff). Some matter-of-factly said they got the standard amount mandated by the company's policy. Mostly, they were vague. Because no one wants to talk about it. There's a fear that the package is tied to your worth. You may find yourself thinking, *At least they're giving me some-thing even when they don't want me around anymore.* This is a slippery slope of self-abasement, as if the Loyalist is still arguing for the company.

BEST ADVICE: Do not tie your value to the severance package. It's a negotiation, not a value statement. That's why lawyers exist: to negotiate without your emotional filter.

There are different "next" scenarios. One, where you're escorted out of the building by Security. Two, where the HR person helps you wrap things up for the day. A third, where the current period is designated as a "notice period" of thirty days for you to get your affairs in order. A fourth, where there is no HR person and you're left on your own to find the exit. There are actually a number of different scenarios based on company culture, policies, and your level within the organization. However, regardless of the bone structure, the carcass is the same. You're on your way out. You've been dumped.

From this point forward, several things can happen:

- Women return to their office and see it as an empty space and not their domain.
- They decide who will be the first person they call.
- They call a lawyer or decide not to.
- They pack up their personal items.
- They wonder how to tell the staff, and some don't bother.
- They walk out the door without making eye contact, or making searing eye contact.
- They realize there are a number of tactical steps they need to take that they have not taken in a while, have never taken, or don't remember how to take.

9

All these decisions and realizations are popping like fireworks while women are still in the throes of trauma. Jenny's story is particularly wrenching. Listen to this. . . .

Jenny had worked for twenty-three years for the same publishing company, joining the firm straight out of high school. She had worked her way up through five promotions and was running a division when the company was bought out by a larger corporation. She had been through acquisitions before and had always survived. At one point, she was the only survivor in a department gutted of twelve other people. "Why did they keep me?" she asked her boss at the time. The boss said, "You never lay off the good ones." This phrase would come back to haunt her deeply.

A few months after the company's acquisition, a different boss, who had always been friendly, called her into his office for her midyear review which she figured would be like every other review: exceptional and complimentary of her high regard within the company. She had superior reviews going back twenty years. She settled into the meeting and within minutes, the discussion veered toward her salary. "You make a lot of money," her boss said. It was a dissonant moment. She had been "working her butt off" and was taken aback.

"Yes," she agreed, "I do make a lot of money," but she wasn't going to apologize for this. She was proud of her compensation; in fact, she felt her worth was greater than what she was being paid. "I work hard," she said. "I've been here twenty-three years, and you know you can count on me to help anywhere in the organization in a crisis since I've worked in so many different departments."

About four weeks later, her boss called her into the company's conference room. The HR person was sitting next to him. Her boss said, "We appreciate all you've done for the company. Today is your last day."

"I was flabbergasted," Jenny said. "I was so angry. A feeling of intense hatred came over me. He had betrayed me. He had set himself up as my supporter, saying things like 'I'm talking to you as a friend, not a supervisor.' After watching me sit there with this news, he said, 'You probably don't believe this, but I really wish you well.' I was speechless. I couldn't formulate words. 'Do you want to take a minute?' he said.

I had given blood, sweat, and tears to this place, and this is how it all ends? I thought. I went back to my office with the HR person whom I had known for quite some time. She said, 'You don't have to stay any longer. We can send you your things.' I think she was trying to be kind, but at that point I couldn't tell. My radar system had shut down. I don't remember the next moments too well. I put things in my handbag—pictures of my daughter, my wedding, things of personal value. I kick myself now that I didn't take more, but all I wanted to do was get out and not make eye contact with people.

"I remember leaving the parking lot, driving away, and then pulling over, totally losing it. My career had come to a screeching halt in a matter of forty-five minutes. I was totally unprepared, totally blindsided. Now all of a sudden I was out of work. Not needed. I was lost. I had a young child, a husband whose salary couldn't support three people and a mortgage. I hadn't looked for a job in seven or eight years. Every once in a while, I would dust off my résumé. But I didn't know how to see myself or even define myself. I didn't know who I was professionally. I had worked three hundred percent!"

This was just the beginning for Jenny. We'll hear more of her story and how she did the hard work of thinking through her professional identity and ending up in a better place.

CHAPTER TWO: THE NEXT TWELVE HOURS

Coping in the Dark

From this point forward, your comfort zone is gone. You're in the outlaw zone. When you return to your office to collect your things, you will be struck by how similar it looks to the way it did a few hours ago when you were still its official owner. Now you're not.

When you call the two or three people you need to talk to—husband, wife, partner, attorney—you will hear yourself describe for the first time what just happened to you. "I was called in by the boss who told me I am being replaced . . . I was let go . . . I was fired . . . I was told today is my last day."

The first person Jenny called was her mother. "My mother had lived through twenty-three years of my career at the publishing company. I needed a woman who could relate to me on that sensitive level.

"My mother said, 'I'm so sorry.' She just listened. I knew my husband wouldn't do that. He'd start yelling about the a**holes, and I didn't want to get more angry. I wanted to let go of it. To this day, I've never told my husband that I called my mother first."

BEST ADVICE: Don't add drama to your trauma.

You will experience the trauma all over again as you say the words and they hear them. According to the *Oxford English Dictionary*, trauma is an emotional shock following a stressful event or a physical injury. Synonyms include distress, stress, upheaval, pain, anguish, suffering, upset, heartache, heartbreak, and sorrow. It's an indelible imprint that can't be erased. You hear it, feel it, experience it over and over again each time you talk about it.

You are not obligated to be a good-girl employee and handle this the same way you would mitigate conflict in your firm, putting the company first and yourself second. You do not have to follow a typical pattern of immediately telling the people closest to you, your spouse, partner, even your staff. As Jenny intuitively realized, she wanted to talk to someone who would listen with empathy and help lower the heat on her anger so she could drive home. If someone pops into your head as the first person to call, call them. They may be the one who can calmly hear your story and tell you how sorry they are. They may be the one to remind you that you're the same friend, same colleague, same VIP to them as you were when you woke up this morning. They may have been through it themselves and can assure you they understand what you're feeling. They're not there to fix things, but to remind you of your meaning to them and your value, regardless of your job or ex-job. I remember my own first "telling" moments vividly, and I want to give you peace of mind as you experience what really happens emotionally when you're fired. You're not alone. Don't scare yourself that you don't know who you are. Remember, this is a bona fide trauma. You will return to yourself and rise to a better situation like all of us who found new resilience and new self-worth.

BEST ADVICE: Call a labor lawyer.

One of the most unexpected sources of emotional support may come from a labor lawyer. When we think of calling a lawyer in these situations, we consider this because we want to know if we have a case and can sue to protect our rights. What's surprising is that if you do meet with a very experienced labor lawyer, they know that the first and most critical help you need is their emotional support. Here is Grace's story. . . .

Grace had worked for an international corporation for thirteen years. She had been promoted consistently from the sales force to run some of the company's most successful new business acquisitions, bringing in half a billion in revenue. She was a member of the senior leadership team, though had never been invited into the inner circle of the CEO's cabinet, not for lack of trying. Still, after thirteen years at the company, she was the quintessential Loyalist who felt beloved by the staff, respected by her colleagues, and highly valued by the clients.

For Grace, the devastation of being fired was swift, traumatic, and mind-numbing. She felt sucker-punched and immediately called her C-suite friends for the name of a lawyer. They gave her the first name on their list and told her he was expensive "but a ball buster." That's what she wanted.

When she arrived at his office and walked into his large conference room, she was surprised. The boardroom table was set for two. He explained that he had ordered lunch for them. Grace said she wasn't hungry. She never forgot his answer, which told her more about his experience than any sales pitch ever could. He said, "You have to eat to prepare for battle."

She spent the next hour and a half listening to his stories. He was charismatic and a good storyteller. He had enough disgust for both of them. As she listened to the naked contempt he held for firings like hers, she began to slowly relax and let go of her confusion. "He restored my faith in my own sanity," she said. "This wasn't his first rodeo. I hadn't even been to a rodeo."

He had already been in touch with Grace's company's legal counsel. He laid out the case and what he thought was possible. Before she left, Grace found the courage to ask the one question that had been plaguing her: What could she say to all the people who were asking what happened, who were furious on her behalf? What could she say to them without jeopardizing any potential settlement?

The attorney didn't hesitate: "Tell them the truth. It came as a surprise. It happened abruptly. There was never a written document or warning. It is not for cause." He then added, "You have to remove the taint that you were at fault." The word *taint* threw her off-course. It sounded like *tawdry*, as if it belonged in someone else's dirty laundry. She left the attorney's office very clear that she could no longer rely on Loyalist behaviors, but unsure of what would come next and how she would feel about it and handle it. She felt her questions about protocol were too small or silly to bother the attorney with, and that maybe she *should* know the answers as a leader, but like Jenny, she felt lost. However, being with the attorney whose business exposed him to some of the darkest sides of leadership and human behavior ironically helped restore her faith that she would arrive at a better, more well-lighted space. She had an ally and began to feel safer. She had come to the right warrior.

If, like most company believers, you don't have a labor lawyer, think of your network and those who have held leadership positions near or in the C-suite. They'll have one, believe me. Out of all the women interviewed for this book, 100 percent had been fired at least once and 100 percent *knew* a woman who had been fired. You'll get some referrals.

You may wonder if you need to call a lawyer at all. If you're like Jenny, whose severance was straightforward, it may be unnecessary. However, a lawyer may be able to get you additional benefits you didn't know enough to request. Equally important, a labor lawyer can be your emergency therapist and advisor wrapped into one. If it's too unbearable and heartbreaking for you to deal with the company directly on any matters, the lawyer will do this for you and relieve you of this damaging burden.

While you're considering who to call and how to describe what happened to you, if you haven't been escorted out the door by Security, you will likely return to what used to be your office to gather the items that belong to you, as Jenny did.

BEST ADVICE: Take your stuff. Not theirs, yours.

Some of the women I interviewed didn't follow this advice, especially if they felt they had created materials that the company was using. Legally, if it can be construed as company property, it's theirs, not yours.

Like Jenny, you'll be driven to remove photos of your friends and family as you begin uncoupling from your environment. There's something about leaving the smiling faces of your family and friends behind that feels too close to abandonment.

Whatever you can't carry, have the company pack and ship to you. If you're asked to do this under the watchful eye of Security, you don't need to make small talk with the security guard whose entire family you may know well from years of greetings at the front desk. Focus on yourself and get the job done. Eleanor Roosevelt has something to say about this too for Loyalists: "You must do the thing you think you cannot do."[1]

When Jenny was told that she did not have to stick around and could leave, she went back to her office. "I don't remember it too well. I just started putting photos in my handbag. I had a work phone that I used for everything. I didn't know what to do with my phone. My cell phone number was attached to my identity. I asked them if I could wipe the phone and keep the number. When they said I could keep it as long as I needed, I felt like I still had that portion of me. I left the building. I went out and bought a new phone but kept my number. It meant a lot to me to keep my number. It was my identity."

What do you do when you're working for a small organization where there is no HR or process for disconnecting you from your employer? Here is Laura's story. . . .

Laura (her real name) had a successful, seven-year practice as a civil litigator in the attorney general's office defending state agencies before deciding she wanted to change her career and make a positive difference in the world as a nonprofit executive. She had been active with the bar association, and the opportunity to be the executive director of their foundation landed in her lap. At the time, she had 165 cases and "absolute burnout." She figured she had accumulated enough money to make the switch to a profession and organization that would make her happy.

The morning she became unhappy, she was sitting at her desk, unwrapping her muffin to eat with her coffee as she read through emails and lined up her day. Her boss walked by and looked at her. Then he walked by again and looked at her again. Something was definitely up. Her instinct was dead-on, but she didn't listen to it and kept reading her screen. In hindsight, she said, she realized he was wondering if it was a good time to fire her. There was a full staff meeting at noon. What she didn't know at the time was the purpose of gathering the staff: to announce her successor who would be at the meeting.

At eleven o'clock, her boss called her into his office. Without any introduction, he said, "You haven't made your goal of half a million dollars. You're fired. You have one hour to pack your things and leave the building." One hour? Unbeknownst to Laura, her successor needed her desk and drawer space.

Laura was stunned. *What goal?* she asked herself, thinking, *He never said there was a half-million-dollar goal. This was a start-up.* Was she naive?

"That was never our goal," she said, "and we all know what an uphill battle it is to raise money here." Her boss looked at her, looked at his watch, and repeated what he had said.

Laura went to her office and packed up her books and papers and coffee mug. Because the nonprofit was so small, there were no policies, no Security to walk her out the door or even confiscate her muffin. She called her partner at the university where she worked and left a message with her partner's assistant. "I've just been fired, and I have no way of getting home because you have the car. Can you pick me up?"

Laura was literally kicked to the curb. She had nowhere to go until her partner could free herself from her classes, four hours later. Laura's experience as a litigator in the attorney general's office suddenly kicked in and reminded her of who she had been before her boss had abruptly upended her life. "As a lawyer," she said, "I wanted to have the last word." Her emotional muscle memory guided her next steps, which is a phenomenon that many women experienced in the moment of being fired.

Laura went uninvited to the full staff meeting that her boss had convened to announce his new plans and introduce Laura's replacement. The meeting had been set weeks before, and Laura, like Grace, realized the decision to fire her was made long before this moment, yet no one had said a word. Laura stood in the back of the room and stared at her boss for forty minutes, silently daring him to announce to the staff what he had just done. He never did. He never introduced the new face in the room, and conducted business as usual to a perplexed audience. Laura left the building and waited for her ride.

Her partner dropped her off at home and went back to work. The devastation was complete. "Confidence wasn't even in my vocabulary," Laura said. "That was the most brutal day for me, and she went back to work. We didn't talk about it until months later."

The disturbing emotions that flood through a woman who feels betrayed, manipulated, foolish, humiliated, or just lost transform rapidly once again as her first night of being cut off from her professional world descends.

Grace was anguished to find herself in a whirl of dark emotions, twelve hours after she had been told there was no place for her in the organization to which she had devoted more than a decade of her life's work. Paranoia headlined her evening, as she talked to herself to try to understand why this had happened, but instead she heard herself through a storm of hurt, demanding to know. . . .

Who betrayed me when I was frustrated?

Who else knew my head was on the chopping block? And didn't say anything?

Who whispered in the boss's ear that someone else could do a better job for less money and they knew just the person?

Who's lying? Who's a snake?

Her rage became a forest fire. Then it died down, and she felt like she had a smoldering, flesh-eating bacteria under the still-numbing effect of the news. Her sucker-punched ego was swollen and sore. She could not get around the image of her boss saying that today was her last day. Traumas are not easily digested or diffused. They take time, like recovering from very bad food poisoning, or any kind of poison that's just entered your psychosphere.

BEST ADVICE: Be okay that it's going to be dark for some time.

Darkness has its serious, no-exit side. At least two women interviewed for this book considered extreme acts to end their pain. We don't want to dwell in these depths, but acknowledge that they exist. One of the first books I read about a firing experience, written by a man, used the word *suicide* on the tenth page. Another man had a psychotic breakdown and was institutionalized after being let go. One of the women I spoke with had fantasies of ending her torment by walking in front of a car. The reason this book was written and is now in your hands is to help you see clearly that your being fired without cause is *not* about your value and reason for being on this planet. Once you're outside the system—away from the company's theater that made you feel less than you are—you will actually have a better chance of reclaiming your personal power than ever before. There's no way of instantly getting around feeling bad about callousness, disloyalty, and rejection, even if you have a highly disciplined spiritual energy. It's okay. Let it happen and know that this is a form of detoxification.

BEST ADVICE: Have compassion for yourself, aware that you are in a discordant state of anger, resistance, and sorrow that is not permanent.

CHAPTER THREE: THE MORNING'S WAKE-UP CALL

You've Been Outed

The first time you wake up without the routine of rushing to the office is eerily lonely until you check your texts and emails. When Grace checked her phone the next morning, she realized immediately that she had been "outed." The announcement of her departure was her first public moment. The cascade of calls and emails came in from all over the company like a rising tide of hysteria. While she knew they were meant to be helpful and supportive, they tested her capacity to remain emotionally neutral.

She felt as if she had been swept up in a new marketing program where she was the product. She had metamorphosed into a brand that she had to protect, as she read the messages from her colleagues reminding her of who she had been to them. Maybe it was that last word of advice from the attorney about being tainted, but she felt her reputation was on the line. Actually, it was more than that. She didn't know which "Grace" she was going to be: the stoic professional, the optimist, the realist, the comforter, the fighter, the bewildered, or the survivor. Because of her uncertainty, she knew she needed to be careful about how she responded, if she responded at all. She could picture her colleagues in their offices at the keyboard or scanning their emails on their phones, as she read:

"Wasn't there another way?"

"This is not the gig I signed up for."

"Time for me to go."

"I'm heartsick."

"What happened?!"

"Thinking of you."

"We miss you."

She was surprised by those who wrote so quickly and by those who didn't reach out at all. This can be one of the most telling rites of passage for Loyalists. Rites of passage "strip individuals of their original roles to prepare them for new roles."[1] Even when the firing happened five years ago, women remembered who they had never heard from and how, in a flash, their opinions of the no-shows changed and their view of the past changed.

BEST ADVICE: Take comfort in the beautiful emails and cards you receive that confirm you made an impact on people's lives.

"There were people who I thought cared about me who fell off the face of the earth," said Jenny. "I had gone to their families' parties and thought we were close, but I never heard from them. Then there were people who reached out to me to tell me how much of a mentor I was to them, and I thought, *Really? I thought we were just talking.*"

Some women received calls from around the world. Some heard from long-ago colleagues who somehow heard the news and asked how they could help. This is a rare moment of clarity about your journey and theirs—the people you worked with day after day and the people you've influenced in some way. Embrace this passage as the special time that it is: an authentic outpouring of support for the contributions you've made to their lives. The curated corporate recognition doled out by employee engagement programs is a thing of the past. This is real and revelatory.

Let's pause to look at the concept of "work friends." Is there really such a thing? High-performing Loyalists often feel they have groups of them. The Gallup Organization knows why. Gallup began by conducting public opinion polls and is now known for its management consulting, particularly related to employee satisfaction. Annamarie Mann, Employee Engagement and Well-Being Practice Manager at Gallup, is the author of an article entitled, "Why We Need Best Friends at Work." She writes, "I'm going to pose a question that is among the most controversial Gallup has asked in (our) employment engagement research: Do you have a best friend at work?" Annamarie was surprised that this question drew so many strong reactions from clients and was willing to concede that some people do not like to meld their personal and work lives.[2]

Perhaps they're the ones who have figured out that all the talk about "work friends" and "family" to which Loyalists devote their energies is geared toward helping the bottom line. Is this misplaced cynicism? As Annamarie cheerfully writes, "Truth be told, Gallup wouldn't have included the item in our employee engagement survey if it didn't lead to improved business outcomes."

With all the data that Gallup has collected about women in the workforce and a culture of friendship and inclusion, the company fails to acknowledge why people have such a strong reaction to the question about having a best friend at work. It conflates employees' emotional health with the health of the company. Employees' hearts and souls are their own. Perhaps Gallup should pose that question to high-performing Loyalists who have been fired and never again hear from their Gallup best friend the moment they are escorted out the door.

In 2019, WeWork, the shared-space company for (mostly) millennials, announced that it was expanding into residential real estate and education as WeCompany to have a bigger influence on workers' lives. David Heinemeier Hansson, the cofounder of Basecamp, a software company, describes the cultish reverence for work and the lack of barriers between personal and professional lives as "grim and exploitative."[3] Writes Erin Griffith for the *New York Times*, "It's not difficult to view the hustle culture as a swindle. After all, convincing a generation of workers to beaver away is convenient for those at the top."[4] In the world of "toil glamour," Gallup's "Best Friend at Work" question seems almost coy.

Of course, friendships do develop at work, and if the relationship is based on more than the day-to-day grind at the firm, these friendships will survive. If the two of you spoke about interests other than the company, the friendship has a fifty-fifty chance of enduring. Stay tuned for more insights on "work friends" in the chapter on triggers. For now, listen to Lidia's story. How many of us have called our company our family?

Lidia worked for a management consulting company for thirty years as an executive. She was first-generation Latina and brought her loyalty and love of family to her work ethic. "I was as loyal as forty dogs you'll ever need," she said. She worked hard to achieve a vice presidency in the compliance division of her company. She was friends with everyone, went to their weddings, their children's graduations, their families' funerals, and the annual reunions of the retirees. Most of us have had Lidias in our professional lives. "My job was as important to me as my family," she said. "It was my love, my business. I was true blue one hundred percent. I told them, 'Just tell me what I have to do and I will do it to perfection.' I was beyond devoted to my job and ran it like it was my own business and the people were my family. I was much too trusting. I believed that if I were the perfect employee, it would work out." It didn't.

"At my company, I was increasingly being asked to let someone go because an executive disliked him or wanted someone new. It was very disturbing. I tried to do what I could to head things off. I would sit down and talk to the employee and ask him to take courses to improve one thing or another. It never made a difference. I had to fire two outstanding performers because management didn't like them."

When I asked Lidia what happened to her, she said, "I can't talk about why I was fired, but the reason was manufactured since they needed to get rid of me. I had seen too many terminations and unjust firings and knew too much. The whole experience was a punch in the stomach. They fired me for performance which I prided myself on. I was fifty-three and had been promoted in every job because I'm a true performer. The cut went very deep. I woke up when this happened. But it was there all along. *I just didn't see it.*

"I lost my soul and went into an extreme depression. I was going to lose my home. I spent many dark nights crying my eyes out and asking God, 'Why is this happening to me?' My faith is very strong, and I prayed every night asking why. Then I was in a bad car accident and when I was in the hospital, they discovered I had suspicious lesions on my spine. I thought, *I'm the breadwinner in my family. I have to work at getting better. I'm going to hunker down with my faith and refuse to accept this.* I went through so many tests after that, and finally, after four years of treatment, they said I was clean. I had been going to a new job during those last two years; it had taken me a long time to find something, but I never gave up. I took a demotion because *some* money was better than no money. My commute was very long, and I used to live thirty minutes from my other company."

As a devoted, spiritual person, Lidia placed her trust in her faith, fervently believing that she would learn how to put herself first and regain the psychological and emotional strength to become her own person and reclaim her future. It took seven years for her to regain a vice presidency at her new firm. In the process, she was profoundly changed. She was no longer "as loyal as forty dogs you'll ever need." In fact, without the pull of loyalty and deep commitment that had filled her days at her other firm, there was "so much less stress," she admitted. "Before, I was too close to the people I managed. Now I'm more relaxed," she added. "There's freedom."

In "How to Detach Emotionally from Work," Kristin Wong writes, "It's quite possible to be too emotionally attached to your job." The results of a 2014 study on the effects of emotions on problem-solving tasks, published in *Frontiers in Psychology*, are eye-opening. "'Participants in a negative mood performed worse than participants in a positive mood but both groups were outperformed by the neutral mood reasoners.'" Wong concludes: "Indifference may be underrated."[5]

Rachel, who worked her way up the ladder to be a global marketing head at two major banks, learned early on about the psychological danger of confusing the personal and professional and believing in loyalty. Unlike the majority of the women interviewed, Rachel had never brought her family photos into the office. Her office walls were covered with the company's abstract paintings. When she was let go from one of the banks, she didn't have any personal mementos to take with her. It was all at home. When asked why, she said, "I didn't want people in my business."

Rachel is able to laugh about the way she was fired from her last banking job. She had a young, privileged boss who was at the squash court more than the office. The day he called her in to let her go, he explained, "I'm not making my numbers. I have to look for ways to reduce costs. In anticipation of my getting asked to make cuts, I've decided to eliminate your position. Well, there I've said it." He grinned at her. Then he blurted out, "This is stressful for me. You know what I do when I get stressed?" He promptly vaulted into a handstand against the wall.

"Are you f***ing kidding me?" Rachel screamed.

Rachel walked out of the building and never looked back.

Trust me, Loyalists, once you hear enough stories about absurd firings, nasty departures, jarring dismissals, and other forms of dark leadership and backstage behavior, it should make you feel great about your own integrity and purpose.

The moment you are no longer a member of the corporate community, you are on your own journey. You will get used to trusting yourself. This is a process. Be kind to yourself. It's an empowering feeling, especially when you are asking, "What just happened to me?" Laura's positive affirmation after she was suddenly dropped from her nonprofit position is worth sharing: "It didn't make sense. It was irrational. There was nothing to do about that. I had to divert and find something else to dive into."

CHAPTER FOUR: TECH HELL

Shocking Realizations about Your Perks

According to the international market research company DMA Research, more than 50 percent of people have held the same email address for more than ten years.[1] Grace had used her company email address for thirteen years. She used it for everything, in spite of being warned. Her attorney had explained to her that her emails were the property of the company if they were on the company's server. They could download them without Grace's permission or her knowledge.

Grace's realization about how much she had been integrated into the company as a senior executive with all of the perks of company-sponsored technology and devices struck her with hurricane force after speaking with her attorney. In less than twenty-four hours, she had experienced fury, despondency, fear, and anxiety, and now she had to take practical steps that required focused thinking. She said, "It felt similar to when my father had just died and I had to meet with the funeral director, and he asked me if I had written an obituary. The deadline was in two hours."

With a sickening feeling, Grace realized that she had been talking, texting, and emailing on the company's phone since the moment she was let go. The company had access to all of her words. Grace had what's known as a "managed" phone. If you own a managed phone, it may not matter, assuming you've been communicating neutral messages.

Or, like Grace, you may find yourself swimming in a bouillabaisse of panic, dread, and obsessive angst with no one to talk to because you don't want to use your managed phone.

BEST ADVICE: Divorce yourself immediately from the company's devices and take custody of your contacts.

Here are a few things that might happen while you're bushwhacking through tech hell. This assumes your company has not stopped your access but is giving you a grace period to transition.

- You have no way to back up your phone since you also have a managed laptop. (Buy a laptop or an external drive immediately. Back up your phone.)
- You've changed your phone number and no one can reach you. (You can ask to keep your old number, like Jenny, but work with your service provider to make sure it's 100 percent yours.)
- You realize you own not one bit of technology that the company hasn't paid for and can't monitor. (Send it all back.)
- Your Apple ID is your company email. (This is fixable; in fact, it's easier to fix than it used to be. Don't search the internet for out-of-date horror stories. Just go online to Apple and follow the instructions.)
- Your gazillion apps are registered to your company email. (You have to change your logins and passwords, one by one, including your Netflix which you need for your calm-down binges.)
- You are worried you will turn into the woman across from you at the Genius Bar who is complaining she's been there all morning after being there all morning yesterday and still can't do blah, blah, blah. (Don't go back.)

A little over twenty-four hours after Grace was let go, she was buying a new phone and choosing a new phone number. She wrote the new number in three different places so she could remember it because it felt so alien to her. Then she started blocking calls from people who were trying to reach the person who used to have the number that was now hers. It was an identity mash-up. "I couldn't help feeling that who I was had suddenly been ripped out from under me. Then I couldn't believe I was so shallow—that my sense of myself was so tied to my job. But I had been with the company for so long. I had let them envelop me, and every bit of technology I owned belonged to them. The company even owned my phone number, my lifeline to the world. They *owned me.*"

Grace had a moment of sudden, deep loneliness, walking alone in the afternoon in the city, imagining everyone in her company was at meetings or rushing to make deadlines while she was blocking unwanted callers on a strange new phone.

When you know your emotions can't be trusted, or you need an instant reframing of your thoughts, call the person who will not add drama to your trauma. This is not the time to worry about imposing. "The idea of people enduring life's challenges on their own is misguided," noted Ama and Stephanie Marston in *Type R: Transformative Resilience for Thriving in a Turbulent World.* "Although we may assume that we're alone in our struggles, the reality is that nothing is more universal than the experience of stressful life events."[2] The Marstons conclude that connecting with and depending on others is one of the building blocks of resilience.

A famous actress known for her drama on and off the screen once said, "It's the friends you can call up at four in the morning that matter."[3] Call them. Listen carefully to how they reframe what is happening to you, or simply listen to how they listen to you. If you have a therapist, check in with them. These moments are therapist-worthy. If you're not ready to speak with anyone, your go-to comfort strategy may pop into your head, whether this is writing in a journal, listening to music, running, watching Netflix, or something else.

A favorite colleague said to me, "If your book tells me how to get through this quickly and easily and without stress, I'm down for that." I'm sorry, but there's nothing quick and easy about this. There *is*, however, an extraordinary gift that comes to you in greater and sharper lucidity along the way. As Jenny, the publishing executive, said after being let go from a twenty-three-year run at her company, "I would never have moved on, never have found myself again if not for this process. I really didn't know what I had to offer outside of my company, what I brought to the table. Would I tell anybody to go through this kind of process? If you're okay, would I tell you to undergo this kind of turmoil? If you have to move on, yes."

BEST ADVICE: Don't judge your career by the last twenty-four hours.

PART TWO

Being Faux-Fired and
Other Involuntary Departures

CHAPTER FIVE: THE LONG GOODBYE, THE SETUP, AND MORE

Six Scenarios to Avoid

I intentionally began this book with the most shocking scenario: the story of a hardworking, long-standing senior executive, happy and successful, who was suddenly asked to leave and didn't know that this would be her fate. Unfortunately, I found plenty of other women who shared this experience. They were fired without cause after a history of excellent reviews and promotions. But as I interviewed more women, I became aware of other scenarios that, in some cases, were even more painful, botched, or just plain sketchy. I want to familiarize you with these situations so you can take steps to avoid being caught in these traps. Pay attention to any similarities to your own circumstances or tuck them away for a later date when your subconscious might retrieve them as a way of preparing you for doing the hard work required to step into a new future.

I offer my "Best Advice" for each situation, but I know you will have your own thoughts about what you would do if you found yourself in any of these six scenarios. Write your thoughts down so you can harness their power if and when you need to remind yourself of your own worth.

Scenario #1: The Long Goodbye

Arlene (her real name) worked for a college in their external affairs department. She was the vice president and had been recruited by the chairman of the board who retired a few years after Arlene assumed her position. He had been her sponsor and her mentor. He had always had friction with the president of the college, and now that he was gone, no one stood between Arlene and the president.

The signs that Arlene should have been seeking other employment began almost immediately. (These signs are the first steps of being "faux-fired," explained in the next chapter.) Someone new was hired between Arlene and the president, meetings were canceled, and Arlene couldn't get her goals and her programs embraced or approved by the board. This went on for more than a year, taking different and more creative forms of pushback. Arlene knew her days were numbered. She said, "I saw the writing on the wall and '*decided*' to retire." But she also wanted her health care coverage. She resolved to stay for three more months after announcing her retirement so she could keep her benefits as long as possible.

Those three months were more detrimental to her health, mentally, physically, and emotionally than any company-sponsored benefit could justify. She remembers, "At the time I thought I could do it, that it was a benign decision, but it wasn't. The bullsh*t that drove me to retire got worse, and I grew increasingly angry and frustrated and couldn't keep my mouth shut. I started telling my 'allies' on the board the truths that I thought they needed to know. Then one day I heard that someone from the board had told the president and his staff that I was toxic and creating a toxic environment. That was the end. No one spoke to me after that; no one contacted me at all. I stopped going to the office, and no one missed me. By that time, I felt like I had no skills, no experience, and couldn't manage myself out of a paper bag."

> **BEST ADVICE:** If you decide to stay for a period of time after you announce you're leaving, negotiate a virtual role that keeps you physically and emotionally away from the office and out of trouble.

Scenario #2: The Heads-Up

Vanessa was told in confidence by someone in the CEO's inner circle that she was going to be let go at the end of the month. This gave Vanessa time to prepare. Except she wasn't exactly sure *how* to prepare. She could update her résumé, start contacting her network, line up a lawyer, and take all of those workmanlike steps. But she wasn't sure at all how she should prepare to feel on the day she was actually told it was her last day. And what about her staff? She couldn't tip them off because she wasn't supposed to know. Vanessa decided to work harder to finish a number of key projects. Why? you might ask. The company didn't care if she finished up her projects. But she hadn't come to terms with this. She was still being the good-girl employee. The heads-up served only to make her anxious and more insecure about whom she could trust. On the other hand, it alleviated the guilt of the confidante who told her. Vanessa found herself comforting him! No, no, no . . . take time off, Vanessa. You're going to be sitting in your office watching yourself not being invited to meetings, or worse, training your replacement who suddenly shows up in your office because she's been assigned to "help" you with a project.

> **BEST ADVICE:** Look in the mirror and confront your denial. If someone gives you a heads-up, use your time to find a new position, not work harder to reverse the decision that's already in play.

Scenario #3: The Setup

Eliza, who worked for a management consulting company, was matrixed with two bosses: her client and her supervisor at the consulting company. One day she showed up early to a meeting with her client and unwittingly interrupted him interviewing her replacement. Flustered, the client admitted that he had requested a change. Eliza knew that she and her client had been on opposite sides of business issues, but she thought this was part of a healthy debate to get to a higher level of quality. Apparently not. The client had made up 80 percent of her business within the consultancy. Eliza's supervisor told her to find another client base in the company, per standard procedures. This required presenting herself and her credentials to other vice presidents in the company who knew her client had fired her. They didn't want to take her on. After two months, Eliza's boss asked why she hadn't been able to find new business. Was she really looking? Was she making the connections she needed? Meanwhile, sensing they were on the losing side, Eliza's staff started to abandon her and latch on to other vice presidents whose positions were secure. When the final word came down that Eliza had been given every opportunity but hadn't taken advantage of the company's largesse and must now leave, she was angry and ashamed. The shame kept her quiet. She tried to gain perspective, knowing that what had happened was the nature of her business, but still thinking she was at fault.

BEST ADVICE: When it starts to feel like a no-win situation, no matter what the leaders are telling you, trust your gut and negotiate a dignified exit.

Scenario #4: Inertia

Maria fully acknowledged that she had been coasting for a long time before she was let go. Her job hadn't challenged her for a while. Yes, she admitted, she should have been looking, but she wasn't. Maybe it was because she had been let go once before when she had only forty dollars in her wallet. It had taken her a year and a half to get back on her feet, and when she did, she focused on building up her savings, her nest egg, in case it ever happened again. She never wanted to be that broke again. But she was unhappy. Still, she did nothing.

Maria grew increasingly complacent, and when new leadership came in, she was let go. When she learned she was no longer wanted by the company, it hurt twice as much. First, because she blamed herself for knowing the truth that she should have been actively searching, and second, because she hadn't been able to make her voice heard above her colleague's when she realized there was room for only one of them at the top. She hadn't managed up well at all. Even through her unhappiness, though, she knew she had outgrown her position.

Maria had a five-month window to disconnect from her company. At first she thought this would help with her transition, but she soon discovered, like Arlene, that being in a place where you're no longer wanted is unhealthy. In the beginning, she reported to her office every day to work on her projects. She left with personal items in a canvas bag almost every evening. In the last few weeks, she went to the office once a week. By the time she shut her door, she felt as vacant as her office.

Maria was offered the services of an outplacement agency and used these to reframe her thinking about herself and her goals. "There were a lot of people coming in and out of the agency from big corporations: technology, pharmaceuticals, banking, retail. Such is the norm for the corporate culture. For me, the new norm is to reposition myself as more than a commodity. I didn't recognize my value before this happened, and now I do."

BEST ADVICE: When you've outgrown your position, acknowledge you can't squeeze back into a role that no longer fits.

Scenario #5: Culture Change

"My mourning started a year before I was let go," Preet told me. "I didn't see the organization keeping pace with the radical shifts in the business. I tried to run ideas up the flagpole, but because there were always new people, there were the same discussions, the same issues, and it was exhausting. The challenge was that no one was looking at the quality of the collaboration and who was accountable for contributing to projects and ensuring their success. Ideas got stymied, and projects became very sluggish. I had forthright conversations with my new boss. He understood the issues but wanted to drive me into a role that would have made me miserable.

"After eighteen years, rising through the ranks in the company, I no longer felt like I was able to add value. I saw it coming. I got layered. I started not being included in meetings, and a new head of the division was hired. Sure, I would rewind the tape and think if I did this better or tried that . . . but I didn't believe in the corporate vision or message anymore. I did look for other positions while I was at the company, but my confidence and energy were zapped because I was exhausted from working around the clock.

"The chips fell as they needed to. When I was let go, it was a relief to me, a welcome change. I decided to take some time off and step back since I had been working constantly. I booked a trip to South Africa. I needed inoculations so I booked a doctor's appointment; it was rare for me to see a doctor, working the number of hours I had been working. About the same time I booked the appointment, I felt a small bump. I was diagnosed with cancer.

"By spring, I will have this behind me. I know I would have put off the appointment if I were still working. I deeply believe that there's some kind of set destiny for our lives. I'm on this particular road for a certain set of reasons, and I'm trying to extract as many lessons as I can. Like self-care. I think women always put themselves at the bottom of the list. We're programmed to put everyone else ahead of us. We need to stand firm and not just accept what's being thrown at us.

"Talking to people who have gone through what I have gone through has given me the kind of moral and emotional support I didn't expect. It's made me step back and refocus on what's important to me.

"I no longer accept the status quo. I've put on my entrepreneur hat and am starting my own business. There will be stress, but it will be different from what I had in my corporate life. Working for yourself is a less risky proposition than when you work for a corporation and the other shoe could drop at any minute. Working for myself is a better strategy for me than setting my future fortunes against the success of a company."

BEST ADVICE: Extracting lessons and gaining resolve from adversity is its own form of self-care.

Scenario #6: The Messy Divorce

Sandra's story has all the drama of a bad divorce: secret liaisons, denials, misrepresentation, people who aren't who you think they are, and irreconcilable differences. When Sandra tells her story, she says she was duped, she had "no inkling of what was coming down the pike," she had no reason to believe her boss would use Sandra's own terms against her. The heartache of this scenario is that Sandra needed to leave, and she couldn't let go.

The story begins with Sandra's amazing success in saving her organization as the newly hired executive director. It took her only two years, but as a self-described "fixer" she was comfortable with "inheriting a disaster scenario" and getting it out from under the happy-go-lucky dysfunction of mom-and-pop management. "Mom and pop" helped her fire the dead weight and bring in a new board chair while they sat back and watched Sandra continue to work around the clock to improve, improve, improve.

The new board chair was Sandra's new boss, and she earned her living as a corporate takeover specialist. She ate companies for breakfast.

Did Sandra see any warning signs? No, because the new boss was effusive about Sandra's knowledge and, with great appreciation (!), sucked her dry in the first six months of all that she knew. Flash to the scene in *War of the Worlds* when the aliens are suctioning human brains for their intellectual property. Perhaps Sandra should have worn a helmet.

While Sandra continued to drill down into the bowels of dysfunction, things happened. Her mother became ill and needed Sandra's help. A new operations person was hired to keep the organization on track. The new boss became beloved by "mom and pop." Sandra began to feel niggled by the endless pile of broken toys. By this time, it had been four years of improvements and Sandra felt she had earned enough goodwill to ask for a more flexible schedule so she could take care of her mom. She let her boss know she wanted to work part-time and eventually transition out of the organization. She reasoned this would be the honorable, easiest way to keep the organization intact, save them money (still fixing), and allow her time to evaluate her next steps. After all, Sandra had worked hard with the board and the staff to foster a culture of fairness, equity, transparency, loyalty, and congeniality.

Instead, her boss fired her. "She handled me like a corporate shark, like a corporate takeover. I was completely outgunned." Unbeknownst to Sandra, her boss had been secretly meeting with the recently hired operations person and talking to "mom and pop." When Sandra pushed back, her boss replied, "But you said you wanted to leave!" Sandra countered with, "Yes, but on my terms." Like a bad breakup, it didn't matter what Sandra said at this point. It was over. What hurt Sandra the most was "to be treated like a child, not like a thought partner. It was devastating."

Like any messy divorce, there's much more to this story than we'll ever know and that Sandra may ever know. Sandra needed to leave and wanted to taper her exit in a self-affirming, humanistic way that she believed was reasonable and deserved. How could she have protected herself from the avalanche of disbelief and despair? What could any of us have done? Maybe put ourselves first, stop trying to save an organization, trust our gut feeling that something isn't right, and finally, walk out the door, as Sandra wanted to do, on our own terms.

BEST ADVICE: There are at least two takeaways here. (1) With a new boss, it's a clean slate, and we shouldn't confuse past success with any guarantees for the future; and (2) It can be fatal to overestimate your worth to an organization. It's better to overestimate your worth to yourself.

CHAPTER SIX: GETTING FAUX-FIRED

When Women Fire Themselves

In most of the previous scenarios, a woman was asked or told to leave by someone else. There is another phenomenon that I discovered where women fire themselves. They are "faux-fired." This is when getting fired is disguised as leaving on your own. The power brokers at the top make it impossible for you to function with any success, so you tender your resignation and leave. Cue the image of the bosses breaking out the champagne. You saved them the trouble.

Barbara, who had been president of her own economics consulting firm, had taken a job as an executive director for a small nonprofit that ran a private rehabilitation center for teenagers with substance abuse problems. Barbara had several extended family members who had suffered through addictions, and she wanted to apply her business acumen in a deliberate, purposeful way. However, after the honeymoon period of three months, it became clear that her leadership was being second-guessed. After the first year, she realized she had been feeling gnawed to death by thousands of emails and comments questioning her decisions. She also noticed a pattern that set her teeth on edge: When she was successful, the achievement was usurped by the chairman of the board. When the chair's ill-begotten plans went south, the failure was splattered at her feet. Still, she persevered because the organization's mission was benevolent and because she was from a generation of women whose persistence in the face of challenges is hailed as strength. As one wise woman observed about this tendency, "Too often, we persist toward unforeseen defeat. We don't know it until we see it."

It wasn't until Barbara learned of inappropriate behavior between staff members, that she decided she'd had enough. Notice her female mistake. It wasn't the disturbing insults they threw at her that made her environment intolerable; it was someone else's disturbing behavior.

Barbara remembers the day she strode into the chairman's office and told him everything that was on her mind. Then she handed him her resignation letter. She had been, for all intents and purposes, faux-fired. When Barbara explains her decision and current unemployment, it takes an hour. Why? She still feels the misery of being a victim. She repeatedly analyzes the bits and pieces of what happened. She tucks in her chest when she says the job was affecting her health, and this was also her fault because she knew what was happening but didn't seek help.

Barbara had a bad case of *defeatist narcissism*. She had always been in control, and therefore all actions, she reasoned, stemmed from her own. Therefore, she owned and dissected all failures. But guess what she didn't see? She was in an organizational culture that didn't value her, almost from the beginning. It was as if she were an alien dropped into a hostile, though at first apparently friendly, culture that became more and more itself as she became more and more herself and exiled to her own otherworld. Captain Kirk would have just beamed up and set a course to a new galaxy, monsters forgotten. But Barbara convinced herself that the organization's culture was aligned with its mission. She wanted it to be that way, and when it wasn't, she pushed harder to make it that way until she made herself emotionally and physically ill. She actually did the best thing she could: she fired herself.

BEST ADVICE: Never abandon yourself to an organizational culture that doesn't value you.

While Barbara's experience became increasingly devastating, Patti, who ran the new business division of an electronics company, had more of an understated, even humorous, faux-firing.

Patti had been called in for her annual performance evaluation by her boss. She had delivered incredible results that year, way above target, and was expecting the discussion to be a recognition of her extraordinary performance. Instead, her boss asked her if she could be "different." She was dumbfounded. She asked what he meant by "different." His answer vaguely came down to "different from the way you are."

When she retold the story to her brother, she realized she was still baffled. Yes, she admitted to herself, she was the one who questioned her boss to make sure he fully understood the ramifications of his plans. Sure, she told her brother, she would ask her boss questions as a way to stimulate discussion, mitigate risk for the company, and (ironically) keep her boss out of trouble. Her brother suggested that Patti write to her boss to confirm what he had said, both for her own clarity and for documentation. Patti did so. Her boss confirmed, yes, he wanted her to be "different." Patti faux-fired herself and is still shaking her head over the absurdity of it. After all, she was a top performer! But Patti knew she couldn't be "different" from who she was; she wouldn't even know where to begin. If that's what her boss wanted for the company culture, she was out.

Mimi had no fewer than twelve transitions in her forty-year career. She had been fired, she had been faux-fired, the firms had folded, or companies had merged, eliminating her position. The worst, she said, was when she was faux-fired. "I had worked so hard and was doing such a good job, and I couldn't believe it but this one guy just didn't like me. He was turning people against me, so when a headhunter called, I went for it. I was crushed. I loved the job I had. Having to leave like that was worse than getting fired because I had worked so hard."

We've all been there. We're the queens of working harder and trying to figure things out, thinking we could have fixed it, if only they had listened to us.

Here's the truth: it doesn't matter.

The main thing you can learn from people who create toxic, hostile, or alien environments is that you are not there to alter their reality. They are on their own journey, just as you are on your journey. You are not inept because you are "different." And guess what else? They don't even talk about you (like you do about them). They've moved on.

At this point, it might be a good idea to read "Why I Am Leaving Goldman Sachs," by Greg Smith. "I am sad to say," he wrote to the *New York Times*, "that I look around today and see virtually no trace of the culture that made me love working for this firm for many years. I no longer have the pride, or the belief."[1]

Culture matters. The leaders who feed the culture matter. As Rachel the banking executive observed, "Cultures can change on a dime. When a new leader brings his own insecurities and pathology with him, the culture changes in the blink of an eye. A corporation is not a democracy. It's an autocracy, a legal entity with boxes for functions that must be carried out. If the leader's point of view isn't 'soft and squishy' and you don't recognize this, watch out." Before Preet decided to establish her own business, she realized that the way she had conducted her initial job searches had a major flaw. "In the past I was always looking for the job at the next level up. I should have been looking at who I would be working for."

Tae Hea Nahm, managing director of Storm Ventures, a venture capital firm, had something to say about culture as one of 525 CEOs interviewed by Adam Bryant for the *New York Times'* Corner Office. "No matter what people say about culture, it's all tied to who gets promoted, who gets raises, and who gets fired. You can have your stated culture, but the real culture is defined by compensation, promotions, and terminations. Basically, people seeing who succeeds and fails in the company defines culture. The people who succeed become role models for what's valued in the organization, and that defines culture."[2]

And you thought it was all about working hard and doing a good job. Welcome to the Loyalists' alumnae club.

PART THREE

Leaning Out: Going Public
One Surprise at a Time

CHAPTER SEVEN: YOU ARE NOT ALONE, A.K.A. THIS HAPPENS MORE THAN YOU THINK

The Stigma of Being Fired Is a Myth

Once you tell people you were fired—guess what? It happened to them. Every woman interviewed for this book knew another woman who had been fired. Some had been fired three times. Could it be if you haven't been fired, *that's* when you should worry there's something seriously wrong with you?

At the top levels, turnover for both men and women is high. Women make up only 5 percent of CEOs at S&P 500 companies.[1] A loss of just one female CEO sends the progress tumbling. In August 2018, *Fortune* reported that CEO turnover was at its highest in two years. "A total of 879 chiefs have been displaced," according to the report. "Most of those changes in leadership were because the executive stepped down, retired, or resigned."[2] Any of those euphemisms sound familiar?

New research in 2018 conducted by academic scholars asked whether women CEOs were more likely to be fired than their male counterparts. Guess what they found? "Female CEOs are 45 percent more likely to be dismissed than male CEOs." This was tied to performance in a strange way: female CEOs were more likely to be dismissed than men when the company was doing *well*. The researchers believe that "gender stereotypes influence board members who decide that the female CEO doesn't have the leadership qualities to continue the success."[3] And there we have the shock of the A+ star performer who's fired when the board decides they need to take the company to the next level, in a new direction, or to new battles to conquer more market share, but with someone "fresh."

Let's get back to your emotions at this point in your journey. Are you walking around as if you have something to hide? Do you think when you look in the mirror, you'll see *FIRED* written across your forehead? Remember, every single person who was interviewed for this book has lost their job or knows someone who has lost their job. Take your own survey of your friends and family.

BEST ADVICE: Don't perpetuate the myth that being fired or faux-fired is a stigma.

Even so, telling others about what happened to you involves more than stringing words together in a prepared paragraph that you rehearse. To help you understand the psychological demons that may be jeopardizing your forward motion, let's revisit the four stages of bereavement that aptly describe the loss experienced by those who are suddenly without a position and a company:

1. Shock and Numbness
2. Yearning and Searching
3. Disorientation and Disorganization
4. Reorganization and Resolution

Because you've always been an overachiever and your go-to position is to take action, you may jump ahead to Stage Four: Reorganization and Resolution, before resolving any of the issues of the first three stages. You think you're ready to go public, and you want to bury the past as quickly as possible. Here are some of the typical steps taken by high-achieving women when they leapt to Stage Four.

- They became engrossed in "comfort tasks." Like comfort food, these tasks made them feel safe and productive. For example, creating spreadsheets of recruiters they needed to contact and articles and books they needed to read made them feel as good as if they'd just inhaled a bowl of meatballs.
- They started segmenting their contacts according to who owed them favors and the people who never contacted them after they were fired.
- They made dates for lunches, coffees, and drinks.
- They began trolling through LinkedIn for connections to connections.
- They began to write a mission statement for themselves.
- They wrote down answers to anticipated questions about their past, present, and future.
- They filled notebooks with ideas and observations categorized as actionable and non-actionable.
- They joined groups, nonprofits, and boards, and became volunteers.
- They fired up the holiday card list, even if it was August.

All of these actions are helpful. Here's the kicker: if you're still angry, feeling totally bamboozled as to what happened, and in need of revenge or validation, barreling ahead may leave you with a few emotional black-and-blue marks on your tender psyche as you struggle to explain to an executive recruiter why you left your firm. But it's deeper than that. As Jenny from publishing says, "You have to go through the grieving process to release the crap you're carrying around. I had to find myself again."

Going public with friends and family is painful but often doesn't involve the same level of theater as going public in your field. The choice of how truthful, how victimized, how you spin the last months of your professional existence is with you constantly. Ignoring that your position has changed is also a choice. How many LinkedIn profiles have you seen that haven't been updated after you know the person is no longer the deputy chief of importance? That's okay. Delaying exposure while still emotionally processing is okay. Eventually, you will want to take control back into your hands, but be advised, chances are your first public performance will be clunky, more like a rough draft that belongs in a bottom drawer.

Nicole had been a high-achieving executive at a software company. She had been promoted several times. While she knew the economic pressures on the company were volatile, and senior management (which included her) met regularly to cut costs and improve efficiencies, it never occurred to her that she was one of the costs that would be cut. After all, they always rebounded and managed to resolve the issues with regularity—ten years' worth of regularity—as they had done just before she was called into her boss's office. When her boss surprised her with a goodbye package with no notice, Nicole's ego was so scorched that within twenty-four hours, she called a recruiter for a position she had passed up just a few months before. She was delighted when the recruiter told her the timing was perfect. Nicole had one day to submit her application letter and résumé for the first round of reviews. Nicole spent all of her time on this: crafting her letter but barely updating her résumé or her story.

When she met with the recruiter, Nicole wasn't prepared to answer the first question: "So what happened?" She hadn't worked at all on her talk track! Her story was full of holes. When the recruiter asked if the boss would be a reference for her, she answered, "Maybe."

Nicole didn't make the first cut, in spite of being heavily sought after by the same recruiter before she'd lost her job. Weeks later, Nicole wondered if she had even been presented.

Nicole's mistake was a teachable moment. Nicole had always aced her interviews, rarely practicing, going with the flow, fending off skeptics with confident answers. Dumbfounded, she realized how badly she'd blown it. Her answer to the question about why she was leaving came down to, "It was time." When the recruiter said that usually people have another job before they leave, Nicole said, "You came to me with this opportunity that was too good to pass up, so I reached out to you," avoiding the question. Nicole knew it was the worst interview she'd had in years and learned a tough lesson. She had acted out of anger and ego, her emotions pushing her to land on her feet as quickly as possible to show the world how valued she was, to exact revenge, and to assuage her insecurities about money, position, and title.

Nicole hadn't taken the time to mourn the professional loss or step back and reflect on whether she wanted to replicate who she had been and what she had been doing or try something completely different. She wanted her professional life to continue as it had been, relegating her dismissal to a blip she could gloss over because she *had* been so sought after when she'd had her powerful position. Her abilities hadn't changed, she reasoned, just her affiliation. She wanted and expected life to continue the same way but at a different company.

Nicole was not about to look herself in the mirror and question what happened, over and over again with varying perspectives, to get beyond the novelty, the fear, and the anguish. She wasn't in full-fledged denial, but she wasn't in full-fledged acceptance either. She didn't see this as an opportunity to explore a new application for her talent, as Jenny did, but as a flash point of unfair treatment. She decided she should work on covering up what had happened to her while focusing on *not* sounding as if she were hurt and blaming her company. Emotionally, however, that's exactly how she felt. How could she explain her situation to others? Nicole decided to practice her story with different recruiters for positions she was not really interested in. It took months and many sessions and recruiters, more than she had anticipated, because she did not have her emotions under control.

At her meeting with a second recruiter who had followed Nicole's career from afar, Nicole said, with little fanfare and too much intensity, "I've left." The recruiter, who had thought she had scored a coup by getting an in-person meeting with Nicole, was startled. Then she began to ask questions, everything assuredly in the cone of silence! Nicole had enough presence of mind to be careful, while she silently tried to pull back her anger, repeatedly drinking water to keep herself from sputtering about how betrayed she felt. Finally, she said: "We mutually agreed to separate," which wasn't exactly accurate, adding, "The CEO had to make difficult decisions for the economic well-being of the company."

Nicole plodded home, kicking herself. She wasn't happy with her performance. Why was this suddenly so hard? It was as if she were an actress who couldn't remember her script because—wait—she still hadn't taken the time to write one she could deliver.

Nicole started to ask for storytelling advice from recruiters she had considered friends. *What*, she wondered, *was the best way to present what had happened to her so that she didn't scare off potential employers?* Interestingly—*not*—they all wanted her to spin a different story. One of them said, "You weren't fired. You stepped down." Remember *that* euphemism from the research on executive turnover? That recruiter continued, "You can say that after many years together you both agreed that for the sake of the company it was time for a change and you worked together to make that happen. Oh, and make sure your boss says the same thing. Don't deviate." Nicole knew herself well enough to know that she tripped over herself when she lied. She would not have "stepped down" if she hadn't been asked to leave. What was the fine line here?

The fourth recruiter knew Nicole and her boss well. She said, "The truth will set you free." She then created the truth. "There were financial pressures. The company needed to cut expenses. The CEO made a choice." Yes, this was true, but why was *she* the choice?

The fifth recruiter promised she would pave the way for Nicole's interview with a search committee and that she should not worry about telling them why she was on the market. When Nicole checked in with the recruiter the morning of the interview, the recruiter had come down with a bad case of amnesia and hadn't told them anything. "I leave that to you to explain," the recruiter said.

By the time Nicole had her sixth interview, she said, "I've moved on and am looking forward to the next leadership chapter in my career.

I was unexpectedly asked to step down after several promotions. The reason I was given was that it was time for a change due to economic pressures. That's all I know." Here's the beauty in this statement: it was true. Nicole didn't know why she and not someone else was displaced. As we learned earlier, she would probably never have a satisfactory explanation. The other beautiful thing about her declaration was this: she told her story in a way that was natural for her. She didn't borrow scripts from other experts, coaches, or books. She took the time to come up with her own words that would not trigger her anger, tears, or neediness. She found the words she could deliver with authenticity and confidence.

Nicole practiced with many, many recruiters and hiring managers, which was an anguished though necessary exercise for her. She had to put in the work and, importantly, come to terms that what had happened to her was *not* just a blip. It was a major life change. It brought with it all the anxiety, dread, uncertainty, and distress that had not been part of her world as long as she had been inside the predictability of her company. It would also ultimately bring perspective, wins, and happiness that could not have been imagined. Nicole didn't realize it yet, but she had passed a major milestone.

By learning, albeit the hard way, that she had to craft and frame her own story rather than borrow words and advice from someone else who wasn't at the same level of emotional upheaval, she had regained a sense of herself and her resilience. In their book *Type R: Transformative Resilience for Thriving in a Turbulent World*, Ama and Stephanie Marston write that "whenever we're confronted with a challenging situation, we [can] give up and retreat into helplessness and defeat, when in fact what may be required is greater effort, more resources, deeper support, or a different approach to the situation."[4] The most telling moment of transformation for Nicole occurred with a woman CEO who was meeting with her for a key interview. When Nicole told her story in her own genuine way, the CEO asked, "How did you cope?" Nicole held her gaze and said, "I knew it wasn't about me. It was about the company and where they wanted to take it." Nicole was offered the job.

BEST ADVICE: Listen to the script in your mind until you understand that your thoughts dictate your reality, and you have the capacity to change both.

While Nicole dove headfirst into personal confrontations to help her navigate her new terrain, other women elected to "volumize" and "get it over with all at once," as if this would make the trauma go away immediately. These women sent email blasts of their new status. You've probably been on the receiving end of this approach. The messages begin: "After more than 8.5 years at [my ex-employer], I will be transitioning to my next professional opportunity. . . ." I confess, sometimes I don't even remember who the women are who are writing me, since I'm clearly part of a giant email campaign merged from old contact lists.

An email blast about the new you is a perfectly appropriate professional step advised by many transition specialists and career coaches. But this leaves out one biggie: the emotional impact. For starters, people you contact may contact you back. Are you emotionally ready to answer their questions? Do you have the stamina to hear their stories of how overworked and underappreciated they are and wish they could leave too, if only . . . ? Are you wearing sufficient psychological armor to resist their probing and be resilient against their judgment? There *will* be judgment. And there will be gossip, as people try to sort out what really happened, so it won't happen to them. Mass communication is a slippery slope if you're still at Stage Three: Disorientation. Suddenly you can find yourself fielding emotional land mines without being prepared for the boomerang effect of volumizing.

Strategic selection of whom to tell and when to tell your story may not appeal to your ego's thirst for endorsement and support, but it can be the best way to gingerly help your battered self. When Grace was dropped from her company, she considered what another woman had done when she "stepped down." The woman had sent a mass email to everyone in her contact list with her new information. On the surface, there was nothing wrong with this, but Grace's guiding principle was to do the best she could for one person: herself. She knew she couldn't physically or emotionally respond to the volume of emails that would come back wishing her well, asking about her plans, and wanting to stay in touch. She trusted her instincts and reached out to the names that bubbled up. And they did. A few every day. Each one of those people represented a relationship she could trust and someone who would make her happier if she spoke with them.

What's important to notice about Grace's approach is that she allowed her instincts to suggest the people she should contact first. She didn't contact the top five influencers or power brokers on her list. She contacted people who had stood by her whether they were in a position of influence or not. Some had been with her through her career for thirteen years. Others had been entrepreneurs in their own careers and, though she wasn't sure at the time why she felt the need to reach out to them, they represented freedom and courage to Grace. Still others were colleagues and bosses from earlier periods of her professional life who knew her well, had stayed in touch regardless of how high they rose, and had a genuine affection for Grace. She also waited to see who reached out to her. One woman, who had worked with her at her now ex-company, called from Europe when she heard the news and asked how she could help. Grace was particularly surprised to hear from a former boss with whom there had been many difficult times. The boss told her she knew of an opening at a competing company and asked if Grace would be interested. Another woman who was on the board of Grace's former company called Grace as soon as she was ousted to say how sorry she was, to tell her she would do whatever she could to help and that they should plan to have lunch on a regular basis. The board member continued to send "How are you?" messages for the next month so that Grace's mornings were less bleak and sometimes outright joyful.

Give yourself time and listen to the messages from your subconscious. What may seem like a random approach to reaching out can actually be self-preserving and strategic. You don't have to do what other people do, flooding the marketplace with forced cheer about your new direction. You don't have to believe that if you're not contacting hundreds of people in your network you're not being resilient. You'll see all those people soon enough, believe me, whether you want to or not.

BEST ADVICE: Resilience requires a pact with yourself.

When you make a pact to reflect on what really works best for you, no matter what anyone else says (including me!), you build core psychological strength that makes you more resilient. You've had a professional trauma, and you need to heal in the best way for you. Whether you're an extrovert, connector, introvert, giver, taker, or any other personality that a Myers–Briggs analysis has labeled you, you're still the one who knows how much you can handle right now and how comfortable you feel handling it.

Let's pause a moment to introduce the unspoken but most critical undercurrent throughout this entire experience: the spiritual impact. I don't mean the religious impact, or the gonna-take-a-miracle-gaze-upward epiphany. I mean the way your inner self is now dealing with this jarring change. I tried to sneak it in when I said *listen to the messages from your subconscious*. Right now you may have a vague recollection of what your inner self sounds like. Remember those self-help books you peeked at while scrolling through your Kindle when you were on vacation? After a week of decompression from your high-powered job, you were actually able to think about yourself and to hear what you were saying to yourself that had nothing to do with a deadline for the office. You were drawn to certain books and feelings.

That part of you is still there, though a bit undernourished from years of being a Loyalist and a get-it-done team player. Here's an example of hard-core conditioning (understandably) blinding the path forward. This was told to me by a college president about a woman soldier, a veteran of Afghanistan, who was newly enrolled in the college. Thirty days before the first day of class, this soldier had been in combat in Ghazni. Now she was on a college campus. She came to class every day dressed in full military gear. After six weeks, one of the veterans who worked at the college gently told her that it was okay to leave her gear at home. For months she resisted. Finally, one day he saw her heading to class with just her backpack of books. He's not sure what made her suddenly agree with him and really see her surroundings for the first time, but he understood completely the psychological and physical baggage she was carrying. It may have felt like protection, but it wasn't helpful to her integration into her new life.

It's okay to listen to your subconscious, your instincts, inner voice, inherent compass, whatever you want to call it, to help you decide how to put one foot in front of the other. The freedom in doing this is that there's no right or wrong according to the rules of someone else's game. This is why as we work through all the small steps surrounding going public, including speaking with former staff and the mother of all public performances—*networking*—it's important to honor what *you* think you should do and to accept that the result will be okay. It's your journey now, not someone else's.

CHAPTER EIGHT: TELLING STAFF, FAMILY, AND FRIENDS

"Rules" You Don't Have to Follow

The accepted protocol, standard business practice, and advice from people who still hold jobs are in full force when it comes to "rules" about how to communicate with your staff after you've been fired. It doesn't mean you have to do any of it, unless you want to. The theme at this phase of your journey and from now on is self—not selfish but self—caring for yourself. And you'll see later how tending to yourself benefits others.

Staff are the collateral damage of your departure. If you've built a team, empowered members of your staff, taken pride in your staff's development, or taken any or all of the steps to mentor talent as the natural leader you are, one of the most bitter pills to swallow is that your team has also been stricken by your dismissal. And the harsh reality is that they are still at the company—coming to work each and every day, occupying the same offices but now without a leader, or with a new leader, and with much trepidation. *What will happen to me?* they wonder fearfully.

When corporate change happens, people operate from their own sense of survival. Your staff is suddenly dwelling in a world of self-preservation. They're anxious that someone is going to come in and clean house. They think, *The boss got rid of her, and maybe I'm next*, especially if they were known for their loyalty to you. Their fear may be so high that if you text them for any reason, even just to check on how a personal issue of theirs has resolved, they won't answer. They don't want to be seen linked to you in any way.

BEST ADVICE: Don't personalize radio silence.

A person's fear about his or her livelihood trumps your relationship. After all, you know each other because of the company. While you may have become close friends with your senior staff, they are still "work friends," and they are feeling like bull's-eyes on a target with the higher-up boss pointing the arrow. They're wondering, *Does the boss have a bigger plan? Is he going to bring in someone else for my position?* As business coach Bob Cooper says, "It's not one hundred percent rational." Your colleagues, the other senior leaders, are also feeling the chill. If it happened to you, it could happen to them—and that may have been the point. Cue: shame is a management tool.

The day Rachel was fired from the bank, she called her senior staff into her office—the office that was already devoid of any personal photos or memorabilia—and told them what had happened in her most unemotional, practiced corp-speak style. When asked what she told them, she answered, "The truth. I told them there was no budget for the plan, the bank had not endorsed moving forward with a modified plan, and they had eliminated my position to save costs. I wished them well. Then I gathered the few items I had and left." Rachel's example stands out from other leave-takings where there was a more protective message. Rachel was true to herself and did not mince words. She *did* go home to share a bottle of gin and Goldfish crackers before noon with her mom, kicking herself for having chosen the company in the first place. But she was done. She knew her departure would create a temporary disturbance, but she also felt her staff would survive since they were corporate creatures used to clawing forward. Rachel's emotional armor kept her from being a caretaker for others when she most needed to be her own caretaker. Sounds alien to Loyalists, doesn't it?

Laura the lawyer turned nonprofit executive had a different approach. She wanted to ensure that her staff felt safe. She asked to meet with them off-site for one last time so she could explain what happened and let them know it wasn't their fault. It's no surprise that Laura's recovery took longer than Rachel's and required extensive, almost manic trips to the gym to exercise away the anger and clear out her psyche. She was still invested in her people, not a bad trait at all, right? That's what we're supposed to do, right? Professional development is a budget item, and we know that anything budgeted is a top priority. Except Laura was budgeted out, no longer with the organization, and the investment-in-others program expired the minute she left the office with her half-eaten muffin. Sounds harsh? Wait for it. . . .

Grace did not talk to her staff at all. She left the company the way a woman leaves a bad marriage. She walked out and never looked back or let them know where to find her. Did this go against her natural team-building and empowerment Loyalist persona? Yes, it sure did. But that first step out of the building was the first step toward creating a new persona. Grace's go-to place was anger. It helped her exit.

No matter how you leave, how do you feel when you start hearing from staff? Staff may ask to speak to you on a weekend, as if Saturday or Sunday is a safe zone beyond scrutiny. Before you take the call, ask yourself, *Why are they calling me? What do I represent to them?* This could be:

- Hope for the future
- Longing for the way things were
- Someone who values them
- Someone who will hire them again
- Someone they can line up as a reference
- Someone who inspired them
- An understanding person not in the rabbit hole
- A source of information about the company
- A source of information about opportunities beyond the company
- A reminder of the good old days

Be careful. You are still struggling with your own emotional fallout. Consider that there is no real benefit to you to bash your company or give advice that could be misconstrued as bad-mouthing the current regime, if this is one of the temptations you're struggling to control. You can say, "I see there will be challenges," then pivot to how exciting it is to look forward, ahead, along new lines, anywhere but the past. Practice your talk track for these calls before you get on the phone, just as you are practicing your public story for the executive recruiters. In fact, try to talk about something else entirely until they get it: you are no longer with the company.

For many senior-level women, there is one person who has more meaning to them than any other: their executive assistant, sometimes called their "confidential executive assistant," administrative assistant, right hand, left hand, the person who makes the trains run on time and who has scheduled every minute of their days for years.

Jenny from the publishing company still has dinner with her administrative assistant. Jenny says, "She was just a sweetheart. I tried to help her as much as I could. I knew she was up against twenty- and thirty-year-olds, and she was having a hard time getting resettled." Could Jenny have taken her with her to a new job? Maybe, if there were an opening, and maybe if she wanted to come. Don't be surprised if inertia wins the day. And try not to personalize resistance, even when you offer to update your assistant's résumé so he or she can move on. Let it go.

As for the young women you've mentored, they're still learning and watching to see what you do. They will seek you out, and when you're ready for these coffees, lunches, and dinners, remember they are still relying on you to model leadership behavior. If you're unable to do this, graciously decline their invitations. If you *are* able to maintain a semblance of their image of you, you will be enriched by the knowledge that you continue to make a difference in people's lives. Relax and enjoy the soothing balm of gratitude.

BEST ADVICE: Remember that the staff you mentored respect you based on what you meant to them at the company. Maintain your decorum.

Of all the people you need to tell, daughters are the toughest. You had wanted so much for them to see you achieve power, position, and prestige. You had done it, and they were proud of you. You heard your daughters boast about you. They made you into a celebrity in their community of friends and teachers and antagonists. You were the rock-solid symbol of who and what they could be, no matter who bullied them or let them down.

And now you were no longer that person. You had toppled.

Grace crept into her daughter's room as if "victim" were the new look. For the first time since being abruptly let go, she began to cry. She didn't mean to. She had thought a lot about how to tell her daughter and had even crafted a good-news story like Mika Brzezinski did when she was fired. Mika walked up to her daughters and said with forced gusto, "I have good news. Mommy's going to be home more often!"[1]

Grace began by saying, "I have something difficult to tell you." Immediately her daughter thought she had a grave illness. This jolted Grace back to a better perspective. Comparatively, getting fired didn't seem so bad. She cobbled the words together to say that the company had asked her to resign. Grace's daughter said what only children can say with absolute earnest conviction, "That's not fair!" She wailed for a long time about how unfair it was, then fell silent. Finally, she asked the most pressing and practical question on her mind: "What do I do with all the swag?"

It will take some distance for you to realize and appreciate that your fall from the top and rise from below is actually more important for your daughter to understand and accept than a straight rocket shot to the stars.

No matter how long it actually takes, it will seem longer as you tell your BFFs what happened and find yourself reliving the episode of your being pushed out the door, tote bag in hand. Your friends are hearing it for the first time, and they care about you. They are in a swirl of protectionism and outrage. For your own sanity, make no more than two of these calls a day and allow at least an hour for each of them.

BEST ADVICE: Pace your calls to your friends.

As time goes on and the memory is less raw and you're in the phase of rebuilding, you may forget to tell friends further down the line. That's okay. In fact, it's healthy. It means getting fired is no longer the central theme of your life. Building your path forward is the theme. The first time you hear yourself saying, "Didn't you know?" and laughing it off will feel like a torrent of fresh spring water bathing your soul.

CHAPTER NINE: ON YOUR MARK, GET READY, NETWORK!

The Truth about Entering the Arena

N-E-T-W-O-R-K-I-N-G

What a power-packed word! If you want to change jobs or you lose your job, *and* you want another one, almost immediately people will ask if you're networking. I recently heard a well-meaning colleague tell her friend, "You have to have coffee with two hundred people." The friend repeated this guidance happily without questioning why. How did two hundred become a magic number? Andrew Sobel, author of *Power Relationships*, says twenty is the magic number, and your "next tier" should have fifty to a hundred.[1] If you're beginning to feel inadequate and kicking yourself for not going to those dreary crudités-filled receptions or online break-out rooms, take heart and read on: there is no magic number. More importantly, pause and consider what you want people to know about your journey and what you want to gain when you engage with them.

Networking is another form of *volumizing*, i.e., mass marketing your new self, whether it's on a Zoom screen or in person. Many people will be curious to hear your story and what you plan to ask of them. Which means you better consider carefully whether you have completed the necessary work to fortify your feelings about yourself and the disruption that has sent your trajectory in a new direction. Without this prep work before you enter the networking arena, you may find yourself saying things about your company that you may regret, complaining too much and too loudly after a few drinks or annoyingly probing questions, or suddenly going mute and losing your social poise when your industry colleagues who know all about your company tell you things about your former firm that you did not want to know. Worse, if you find yourself getting angry all over again, you may end up retreating to those dark corners of your mind, reopening wounds that you had worked so diligently to heal. Let's start with this. . . .

BEST ADVICE: Don't confuse moving quickly with moving forward.

You don't have to be out there on the stage for all the world to see your pain the moment you find yourself without a company. You're not going to walk into a room or appear on a screen and suddenly feel loved again. There's no magic bullet or typical time frame for recovery. A woman who sidled up to me at a luncheon soon after she learned that she was being demoted after fifteen years at her firm looked as happy as a bloodhound who hadn't eaten all day. "What happened?" I asked.

"They brought in someone over me. They didn't even ask me. She's twenty years younger and doesn't know what she's doing. She met with some of my clients. . . ." She regaled me with a detailed account of why the woman should *never* have presumed she had any relationship with these clients, then was about to ask me if I knew of any openings when thankfully we were asked to take our seats. I think it's pretty clear that whatever this poor woman thought she was doing at the luncheon, it wasn't "networking," though she may have thought she was lining up her options and supporters.

When Jenny the publishing executive found herself suddenly out of a job, she said, "Now I'm out on the street, and no one knows me. I haven't had to sell myself in twenty-three years. Who am I? What's my thirty-second sales pitch?" Another woman who had been let go from a financial services company was consumed with what she should call herself on her business card. She said bitterly, "People don't pay any attention to you as soon as you lose your status and no longer have the right card." Ding, ding, ding, she shouldn't be "networking" if she's still defensive and hasn't been thoughtful about what she wants to do next. You know her, right? You've spoken with her, then quickly invented an exit move. You don't want to be her.

Here are some steps you can take to avoid the sad-eyed bloodhound look or bitter defensive plays:

- Before you debut your new status in public, do a deep dive on learning how to value yourself and your time. I talk more about this in Part Four.
- If you can't control the urge to go out and hunt, think quality over quantity. "Networking is spiritually dry if there's not a cultivated relationship," observes business coach Bob Cooper. Be intentional and choose situations where there will be more people you want to connect with than not.
- When people approach you, and you are not ready to include them in your journey, just sidestep any question you don't want to answer. There's nothing written in the post-Loyalist handbook that says you have to answer questions about what happened to you. You can say something as simple as, "Yes. I'm no longer there. How are *you* doing?" Practice changing the subject.
- If people persist in bringing the topic back to your being dumped, stop and think about why they're so interested. Gossip is golden for those who want to show they're in the know. For persisters, excuse yourself with the classic real or digital handshake and just say, "Great seeing you again," then walk away or leave the chat room. You can practice this with your least favorite relative.

- If you do decide to put yourself out there, be focused. Network with a talk track and a plan of what you want to find out from the people you'll be speaking with. It may not even be about opportunities. You may find yourself curious about how someone ended up in their current position, especially if it is much different than their previous role. You may want to know how they got their start in a business and what they are still most proud of achieving. I always felt a conversation had been successful if I came away with just one new idea that helped me think about my situation in a different way.

But let's go back to the point where *everyone* is saying you should let your network know immediately that you're on the market. *What's my network?* you may be asking yourself. *Do I have one?*

You may have had an incredible network within the company that dropped you, but outside of that company, you may feel relatively unknown unless building relationships was part of your portfolio.

Here's the secret about networks: one solid lead is all it takes. You will be amazed how one person offering to make the easiest of introductions—connecting you by email to one other person—can lead to a cascade of helpers. Here's the other secret about networks: you can spend a lot of time crafting emails, collecting introductions, placing follow-up calls, taking promising meetings, and end up with one thing: a larger network. You're busy almost every day with coffees, drinks, lunches, meetings of all kinds, and it feels comforting the way your minute-by-minute old life used to feel. After all, comedienne Joan Rivers's worst fear was to have an empty calendar. But at the end of the day, you may find you haven't been referred to any kind of an opportunity you would seriously consider. Not only that, you can't remember why you connected to so many people on LinkedIn who bill themselves as Joyful Advisor, Impact Thinker, or People Connector.

After the first time she was let go, Rachel the banker joined every possible association board to network and, she later admitted, to fill her days. What happened? She became overwhelmed with committee meetings, hours of make-work, and obligations she dreaded. The positional power and recognition of board work seemed like a faint echo of a familiar song she no longer sang. Eventually, she dropped them all with a thud, recognizing that she had to take time to stop twirling and think about what she really wanted to do next.

Jenny, who had cried despairingly after she lost her job with the publishing company, took advantage of the company's offer of an outplacement service. "I thought I would find work in two weeks. I was clueless. I had no idea how long it would take me. Would it take six months, a year? The direction and structure I got from the outplacement service was direction and structure I was not able to create myself. They helped with tactical steps like rebuilding your résumé, networking, and interviewing skills, but they also pointed out that this was a time to redefine yourself and possibly take another career path. I worked harder in those nine or ten months with outplacement than I had in a long time because it involved emotional work."

Whether you use an outplacement service or other professionals to help structure your transition, it will amaze you how far and wide the professional world will stretch to fit your embryonic self.

BEST ADVICE: The best part of your journey are the people you never knew existed who come to your aid.

CHAPTER TEN: HANDLING NEWS YOU DON'T WANT TO HEAR

Breaking the Habit of Yearning

G et ready. As you heal and steel yourself and think about how you want to go forward and accept that you still have some hard work to do to let go of the twinges of pain and anger that sneak up on you unexpectedly, get ready for company news that explodes your fragile equilibrium. Armageddon is happening, and someone who is unhappily watching it from inside the company is going to let you know. Prepare yourself to regress back to a boatload of insecurities.

BEST ADVICE: If you meet or talk to someone from your past life at the company, schedule coffee or drinks later that same day with someone who represents your new life to remind you of who you are now.

When Molly was cut from a major financial services company in New York City, she was horrified by what happened next. The marketing and communications organization that she had built over twelve years

71

was destroyed in a month. It was split up and reorganized. Once it was fragmented, the budget was gobbled up by warring internal factions. To add to the free-for-all, Molly was blamed for wasting huge sums of money allegedly with no results to show for it. She was devastated.

Two months after Nicole was booted out of her position as the chief strategist for her software company, she heard that the new chief strategist was claiming that none of what she had put in place was the right strategy. She heard herself being accused of not thinking big enough. Nicole knew she had put forward several "big" scenarios, only to have them shot down by the boss. The ones she had managed to push forward, she had done using a tremendous amount of street cred, with guarantees to the boss who demanded that there would be absolutely no added costs. These successes were buried under the new headlines that she was a small, incremental thinker. To finish off the past, the new chief strategist had not bothered to learn the institutional history and was demanding twenty-four-hour turnaround on proposals for "big ideas" that Nicole knew were dead fish. She was saddened by the magical thinking and all the wasted time and talent and destruction of real progress. *This*, Nicole thought, *is how companies run in place.* Nicole had a deep strain of loyalty and ethics. It was difficult for her to look in the mirror and shout, "It's not your problem! Nicole has left the building!"

Grace had the opposite experience. Her company didn't dismantle her legacy. They used everything she had put in place, without changing a thing. Except her. Same strategy, same execution, same time frame, even down to the same location for an off-site holiday dinner. Grace had created a turnkey operation with staff who could produce and were solid performers.

Which is more painful? The destruction of everything you built, or the continuation of everything you built under a new chief who will claim it as her own?

Grace was both hurt and proud when she heard the company was implementing her ideas and using her strategies as before. She had created an operation that could succeed without her. Essentially, her succession plan had worked, which business analysts praise as the hallmark of great leaders. But Grace became confused and self-depre-cating since she hadn't had control over her own exit. *They just didn't like me*, she told herself. This is dangerous. It assumes that those in charge are experts in assessing not only your value, but who you are! *They are not.* They are leaders at a point in time in the company's evolution and their *own* evolution.

You may continue to yearn for news of the company. This is all part of Stage Two of bereavement: Yearning and Searching. For Loyalists, this may be the toughest habit to break, even after you've found a new role for yourself. Here are some tips for tricking yourself into not asking about the place you left behind:

- Delete the company from your news feed. If you can't bring yourself to do this, check on the latest posts *only* when you know they will not send you into a frenzy. Be hyperaware of your reactions so you'll know when this might be.

- Realize that you are in training—emotional training—much like an athlete undertakes physical training to reach her goals. If you're the kind of person who counts her daily steps, keep track of each day that you don't seek any news about the company.

- Resist the urge to have dinner with your old company confidantes. These dinners can be awkward if you find yourself fishing for news and they find themselves unsure about how much they should share with you, for your sake and theirs.

- Realize that some ex-company colleagues will only want to see you if you will tell them what really happened. Suddenly their pressing invitations for drinks subside when you have no further information to give them. Consider yourself lucky.

- Imagine yourself in front of a box of chocolates. You've already eaten one, and now you force yourself to put that second piece back. This is you *not* catching up with people from the company who are dying to tell you what's been going on.

- Talk to your BFF who will stop you from telling stories about the company with an emoji and text that asks, "Did you notice I didn't ask any questions?"

As you venture from your inner circle to tell your cousins, your former colleagues from other institutions, your followers on social media, your book club, or whoever inhabits the far reaches of your 'hood, a funny thing will happen. You will become too bored to go into much detail about what happened to you. You will hear yourself tell people you're not there anymore. Your tone of disinterest and choice of present-tense topics will move the conversation forward, away from the past and your old self. In fact, if you are focused on reframing your situation and able to be upbeat about the possibilities ahead, people will surprise you by saying, "Congratulations! That's great news." This is called *Attitude Power*.

BEST ADVICE: Your attitude dictates their attitude.

At some point, you will begin to realize that the emotional charge of being fired has withered or is gone altogether. Each telling becomes a matter of fact, not feeling, and when someone looks aghast wanting to open a vein for gossip, you realize that the electricity is now buried deep beneath the surface, no longer a live wire, and you honestly can't remember what happened when! God bless occupational amnesia. There's no formula for when this might occur, but for most it does occur, though it's not a sudden development and follows the oscillation of a sine curve. The people from your past, your coworkers, your colleagues will reach out to you and bring you back in time to the scenes you no longer occupy. If you're prepared for the pain, the jolt is less acute each time until it's finally muted.

For Eliza from the management consulting company, the fallout was brutal after her client and then her firm let her go. She was unable to sleep and suffered from a chronic lack of confidence that made her self-sabotage at every step during her new job search. Shame and defeat became her closest friends. "It's been very lonely," she said.

Eliza had to find points of light to break through the gloom and realize that she was no longer meant to be in the firm's culture. Here's a guideline to think about: the amount of time it takes to mourn, then heal, is proportionate to the amount of time spent in a hostile culture multiplied by the lack of people who share your beliefs and core values. For Eliza, it took three years. Once she tempered her anger and stopped telling her story as if it had happened yesterday, she began to steady herself. She also began attracting the right kind of people into her life. Yes, that happens. She realized that the activities she was most passionate about and had previously kept out of the center of her life were in fact what made her feel the best about herself. That's when she decided to take a risk and pursue them as a career choice, not just as a weekend wannabe. She's working pro bono for organizations she cares about and will soon land the right job with the right people. Or not . . . if she holds on to her anger at people and a culture she was never meant to inhabit. She couldn't and can't change that. Move on. They have.

PART FOUR

Preparing for
Your Next Role

CHAPTER ELEVEN: EMBRACING UNCERTAINTY

Changing Your Mindset

How long does it take to find the next, right position? Google will give you answers that range from six months to two years to longer than you expect. But for Loyalists who have been let go or faux-fired, it's more about the journey than the timing.

During this third stage of bereavement, "Disorientation and Disorganization," you will make bold strides forward and be pulled back by old, stale behaviors. There will be moments of joy as you realize that you no longer have to pretend to enjoy your ex-company's puerile team-building meetings, and moments of despair when you face a search committee and realize they're questioning your ability to lead given your "abrupt" departure. But, perhaps for the first time in decades, you have the opportunity to reflect on the life you've been leading, or the life you've been following, if you've allowed the corporate culture to take over your psychosphere.

Early on in my journey after departing from the company I had been with for many years, I had the good fortune of meeting with a very wise man whose advice helped to orient me. He had just left a lucrative position with a finance firm he had cofounded. He asked me how he could help. I was so new to my circumstances I didn't have a clear answer other than, "I'd appreciate whatever advice you can give me and suggestions for people I might speak with, even if it doesn't lead directly to an opportunity." He considered this, then asked, "Do you want to recreate what you've had or do something completely different?"

I was totally stumped. This question hadn't even occurred to me. I knew what I knew and what I had achieved and was just charging ahead on the same highway. "It is our mindset about our own limits, our perceptions, that draws the line in the sand," according to Harvard psychologist Ellen Langer.[1]

Self-reflection and reframing your professional identity probably hasn't been a primary state of being for you. For so many years, you have evaluated yourself based on your short-term and long-term goals for the company, your rise up the C-suite ladder, your positional power, whether or not you closed an important deal, your good day or bad day. You joked about your life in the margins—your desire to find a partner, your newfound contempt for sugar on your latest diet, your two-day-old vacation that felt like it happened a decade ago.

Women will say of women, "We like to get things done," as the highest form of compliment. And you're the woman who worked fourteen-hour days, then went to the gym and answered emails while running on the treadmill.

Now is the time to put that same energy into finding your path forward and creating the life you want to live. After all, you know what it was like to be in your old life with predictable ups and downs. The beauty of this nascent phase is that you have an opportunity to really change your course, not just for two weeks on a vacation, but for as long as you like. To do this, however, we must teach ourselves to be comfortable with uncertainty.

Deepak Chopra, author of *The Seven Spiritual Laws of Success*, writes, "In the wisdom of uncertainty lies the freedom from our past, from the known, which is the prison of past conditioning. Without uncertainty and the unknown, life is just the stale repetition of outworn memories. Your tormentor today is your self left over from yesterday."[2]

"Your tormentor today is your self left over from yesterday." That stings. But print it out and put it on your refrigerator if you're that kind of person, or set it up as a reminder for yourself every morning at nine o'clock if you're that kind of person. Expect slippage, back to your past conditioning. You'll need to be reminded to face forward.

In *The Book of Awakening: Having the Life You Want by Being Present in the Life You Have*, Mark Nepo tells a parable of saltwater fish that were confined to a ten-gallon fish tank. When the tank had to be cleaned and the fish were transferred to the larger space of the bathtub, they continued to swim in the small circle that had been drawn by the walls of their tank. He asks, "What had life in the tank done to their natural ability to swim?"[3]

Are you the Portuguese fighting fish swimming in the same small circle? How do you even *begin* to think differently?

Perhaps you already have. In *Type R: Transformative Resilience for Thriving in a Turbulent World*, Ama and Stephanie Marston write: "Perhaps what we truly long for is an expanded sense of self more suited to who we have become, what we value, and what works in the changing world around us."[4] The idea that we have outgrown the old corporate culture, the goals we used to have, and the routines that were so important at one time is somehow inspiring and threatening at the same time.

BEST ADVICE: Trust that what happened to you needed to happen for you to move forward in your life.

Venturing into the uncertainty of the big ocean is difficult in ways that you have not even acknowledged exist. You're unaware that it's your ego and its steady diet of power, title, and position and its need for recognition that is steering you over and over again to the same pond. As Nicole realized, "It was much easier for me to live in a fantasy land of who I was when I was in the C-suite. Then my ego got slammed, and I realized my fantasy of myself didn't matter. I had to figure out what I had to do to be on my game a hundred percent."

As you struggle to rewrite your journey, you will be constantly tempted and pulled back by the symbols of success of your past travels. You will feel the high, especially as you consider new roles and new offers that come with the trappings of title, power, recognition, big money. That's what companies have at their disposal to reel you in to do what they need done. You will never feel as flattered and desired as during those negotiations to get you to say "Yes!" But the real quest, the tougher "get," is your own happiness. It's not easy to hold out for yourself after years of putting others first, working hard to prove yourself to someone else, and being a reference point on someone else's compass. You won't be "promoted" by a boss to a better, higher position of *you*.

Why is it so difficult to trust a new version of yourself? Think back: What role did you play in creating and feeding your corporate culture? If you were at the senior leadership level, you probably played a key role, hiring and firing with the best of them.

Mark Nepo asks: "In what ways do we shrink our world so as not to feel the press of our own self-imposed captivity?"[5]

In our company's community, we insulate ourselves behind the gates of conformity. Bob Cooper acknowledges, "When you're wearing the badge of the system, you *are* the system." As soon as women (and men) get past a certain tier in an organization, they become the guardians of their self-imposed gated community. Their community is fenced in with marketing materials and slogans and populated by teams and company retreats. Hell, they create the marketing materials, teams, slogans, and company retreats. They churn out an endless supply of corporate narcissism.

Odd things can happen inside the gates of our company community that are not all that healthy. Take, for example, the indulgence of what I've termed "Munchausen management." Munchausen syndrome by proxy is a psychological disorder where a parent or caregiver intentionally fabricates symptoms in a child as a way to gain attention and earn praise for their caretaking. In Munchausen management, leaders create problems for their subordinates that the leaders then solve so they can gain attention and admiration from the community while the subordinates are left weakened and bewildered. It's a "faux-fired" technique—the environment becomes untenable, and the subordinates leave, essentially firing themselves.

It's easy to lose perspective in captivity. This is what happens when people suffer from Stockholm syndrome: they develop "a psychological alliance with their captors as a survival strategy during captivity."[6]

So don't be too hard on yourself when you discover you may have forgotten how to swim. As I said earlier, your skills and talents don't disappear when the job ceases to exist. In fact, skills accumulate to take you to a level you always wanted. "I'm the perfect CEO," reasoned Laura, the lawyer turned nonprofit executive, after consulting for nearly a decade. "If I had stayed with one organization for many years, I would have been way too insular and less willing to take risks. I've gained so much more experience and knowledge from working with so many different organizations."

You can't rebuild until you've let go—a glib statement fraught with uncertainty. But try to summon the memories of when you felt free— before your company became your guiding light and internal metric of value. Jenny Blake, author of *Pivot*, recounts Steve Jobs's 2005 Stanford commencement speech where he asked students to "connect the dots backward" so they could see the genesis of their current position. Blake takes it one step further: "Reflect on your work history and connect the dots to see how you have *already* pivoted from one related area to the next."[7] In other words, give yourself credit for the changes you've already made transitioning from one business function to another. According to a study by the *Harvard Business Review*, Genesis Advisors, and the International Institute of Management Development, leaders have on average 13.5 transitions during a professional career span of more than eighteen years.[8]

Take a morning to spend time with yourself, to walk down the lane of the changes you've made throughout your career and applaud yourself. And while you're at it, isolate the dots that make you smile, that remind you of a time when you looked forward to walking through the door of your company and weren't in the throes of someone else's fraught journey, someone who was driving the bus and making decisions about the right and wrong people to keep on the bus, as Jim Collins points out in *Good to Great*.[9] Once you're ready to trust your emerging version of your professional self, something marvelous happens: others trust you and begin to show up in your life.

BEST ADVICE: Trust that you'll be connected to the right people at the right time.

Deepak Chopra's fourth spiritual law of success is "The Law of Least Effort." This includes accepting things as they are at this moment in time, recognizing that "all problems contain the seeds of opportunity."[10] When you remain open, without judgment or argument or resistance or forcing the result, you will be surprised by the people and opportunities that come your way. If it sounds mystical, it is. If it sounds too good to be true, it isn't. People will come into your life from different avenues. People you viewed as a "certain type" may now be seen in a different, less stark light. You are no longer bound to judgments passed on by others, nor are you trying to maintain the illusion of power. In *The Art of Dreaming*, Don Juan tells Carlos Castaneda, ". . . most of our energy goes into upholding our importance."[11] Imagine if we just accepted where we are in our lives at this moment and just let it be. This is you without makeup.

For most of her consulting career, Laura had people show up in her life who continually moved her along until she had built an international business around a simple concept: teaching people how to ask for what they want in life. She worked incredibly hard at making the most of these sudden opportunities, connecting the dots, connecting people, and driven by a need to help others learn to help themselves. Recently, on one of her business trips, she encountered an individual who proved in a most dramatic style the benefits of trusting that the right people will come into your life. Laura was upgraded to first class on an international flight. She found herself sitting next to a man who described himself as a serial entrepreneur. He told her that he had met the investors for all of his companies by doing exactly what he was doing at that moment: flying first class so a potential investor would sit next to him. In fact, according to *Inc.*, first-class seats and lounges are "the ultimate networking rooms."[12] This is what I would call a *strategic allowance for uncertainty*. It is a better gamble than an economy seat next to your old, tormented self.

CHAPTER TWELVE: AFFIRMING YOURSELF

Techniques of High-Achieving Women

A word about affirmations, two words actually: they work. *You* can be the someone who says to yourself: "You're a hot property, never forget that." You no doubt have experience writing goals for the company or answers to questions from corporate surveys about what makes you all fortunate to work at the company. Now it's time to exercise that muscle for yourself. Sure, it's out of shape and not toned, so start with a truth that can't be challenged, even by you, such as, "I have many years of experience." Then try to answer the question about what makes you fortunate to be you. Tie it all together by making affirmations for yourself. They should sound like you and be easy to remember. Some simple affirmations:

- I am great at what I do.
- I can lead others to achieve great things.
- I am valuable.

For bonus points, make up something so self-aggrandizing that you would be embarrassed to tell anyone you really think this much of yourself. That's your fourteen-karat affirmation.

- I am so friggin' charismatic that when I walk in the room, everyone knows "she's the one."

Just those few affirmations will help stem the tide of "No . . . Can't . . . Why me? . . . Worthless . . . How did this happen?" You get the picture.

If you're struggling with finding the right words for yourself, look back at all those beautiful emails you received or the special letters you kept that had surprised you with their open admiration for your achievements.

BEST ADVICE: Practice telling yourself with absolute conviction, "I'm a hot property. My biggest challenge will be choosing the right opportunity."

You need a reset, and this requires you to sit back and think about the journey you want to take, even if your mind is blank and your heart is aching. The beauty of this: no one's expecting you in the office. You have the time. Here are some of the tools high-achieving women use to enable them to think differently about themselves and their future that can help you step forward.

- *Write a unique value proposition.* Whether you do this or not is less important than the fact that you believe you have unique value.
- *Collect inspiration.* Go out and buy as many notebooks as you think you can fill with ideas, observations, reflections, goals, revised goals, and more. The difference between this and a journal is that you will be collecting anything that enables you to think differently and see the world from new perspectives.
- *Create a vision board.* If you enjoy seeing goals in pictures, try this. We've been told many times that people

87

who actually write down their goals have an 80 percent chance of achieving them. Maybe you're tired of that one-dimensional method. Maybe you need to frame and hang photos that represent your dreams. Start with what comes to mind; don't force it. We'll meet Allison shortly, an executive with a theater production company, who still has her vision board years after she left her company. Allison is now living those dreams.

- *Join outplacement group therapy.* Jenny the publishing executive had a weekly group meeting at her outplacement firm led by a counselor who focused on the emotional preparation for a new role. "I have a pretty thick binder of notes, and it's overflowing," Jenny said. "It tells my tale and what I did and thought at different phases, and I love to go back and read it, even though it's painful. But I don't think I'll ever be at ground zero again."

- *Produce a You Video.* If you're not into pen and paper, cutting and pasting, glue and photos, private journals, or group help, make a video of you telling yourself about all of your fine and exceptional qualities as if you were narrating an audiobook about leadership—or any topic that reminds you of you at the top of your game. This is a dynamic version of facing yourself in the mirror with honesty and conviction. One tip: try to keep it under thirty seconds so you won't feel you have to set aside a special time for viewing. You'll want to watch this clip between any disconcerting conversations or destabilizing moments.

- *Hire a private coach.* We've talked about this before, and the right coach can make a significant difference in your confidence, objectivity, and evaluation of the next best steps for you. They can't stop you from making errors in judgment, and you will. But when you do, they'll be there to talk about what happened, how to recognize signs that it might be happening again, and how to steer yourself away from potential hazards to a better place.

- **Resurrect classics like What Color Is Your Parachute?** First written in 1970, this book has been read by millions of people. One possible reason for its popularity may be just the remedy you need: it is exceedingly clear and instructional about every step you need to take to determine your future. It is chock-full of advice like, "Take an eight-and-a-half-by-eleven sheet of paper and draw a grid along the left side, listing from one to ten the kind of people you like to work with. See Diagram A."[1] For those who need to step outside the world of ambiguity for the moment, this paint-by-numbers approach to the big picture can be a relief.

- **Enlist different people for different kinds of advice.** No one person has all the answers, ever. Even your BFF probably specializes in a certain kind of advice and caring. Others who have been let go have other kinds of advice, and still others may tell you something that never occurred to you. Try to diversify your team of go-tos so there's someone who can counter or empathize with every little thing that may take you down a notch on the ladder of hope. Even if you're annoying your team in the moment, they should be the kind of people who will get back to you once they've had time to clear cache and listen to you repeat yourself, with a new twist.

- **Relieve the stress by venting.** Yes, it is okay to indulge yourself in verbal therapy as long as you: (a) Do this in person or over the phone, but not on your FB, Twitter, and Instagram accounts that live forever in cyberspace; and (b) Give your go-to team a break so they can clear cache, as I said.

- **Change the environment.** Take a long trip. It detoxes you.

- **Postpone going into fix-it mode.** Focus on taking care of yourself physically and mentally, and the reset button will eventually engage.

The amount of time and resources you are able to devote to preparing for the next chapter in your journey will be different for everyone. Someone who has pressing financial needs may be tempted to put the self-discovery work in the margin, especially because it seems like a luxury to spend time reflecting about yourself. This is not a good idea. Even if you need to take a job immediately to pay bills, take time to think about where you've been. Compartmentalize if you have to, even scheduling time in the morning or at night to simply think without distraction. You may feel just fine or find yourself asking, *Why am I bored? What's wrong with me? I'm not the same.* You aren't the same. You've been changed. Be kind to yourself, and remember, even a new job does not have to be permanent. It can be a bridge job while you get yourself whole again.

Others may take a job too quickly, the first job that comes along that pays about the same as the old job and has the same title and status. Be careful. Grace almost took a job like this, ignoring the warnings of all those who had been fired by the boss within months of signing on. The money and title were so tempting. Grace thought it would solve all of her problems. She'd be safe again, her identity restored thanks to her position. Now that she had been through this once, she could take on a tough boss and walk away if it didn't work out. Right? Not really. Grace woke up feeling strong and went to sleep feeling fragile. She spent many hours reflecting about whether she was in denial or seeing clearly. She chose to decline the job offer and strengthen her resolve to recognize and value opportunities that did not have the same characteristics as her previous role. Repeating what she had done and where she had been would have been the easiest, though likely more damaging, path to follow.

Personal transformation coach Shushun Aleaqui says, "The moment the firing happens, you fall out of the system. Some women scramble immediately to go back into the system. Others remain outside of the box. Inevitably, those who don't hear the message the first time they're fired often hear it a second time."

Whether or not a woman sees this as a second opportunity to self-actualize or another knife wound to her value depends on her readiness to begin one of the most important and nuanced journeys of her life.

Nicole, who had been let go from her software company after ten years, had two important allies: her BFF who texted each morning and listened to Nicole's agony throughout the day. And her son, who called each night to deliver uncanny wisdom and spoke to her for hours about her life, his life, and the family. Imagine the bonus of talking with your son or daughter about something other than them? Seriously, when your child can help you and wants to help you, there's so much love in this that you can't help but feel you've done something right. Hold on to that.

In addition to her BFF and nightly calls with her son, Nicole was fortunate to have a workout routine already in place. She knew that stress could take a serious health toll, and she didn't want to add that to her pile of sins. There's even a field of study about this called "psychoneuroimmunology" that researches the health effects of your state of mind. Now don't Google this and get anxious about being stressed, just go for a walk or do something that is physical rather than cerebral.

This may also be a good time to learn more about actual nutrition and the schemes of the giant industrial food complex, which may provide the fodder you need to discharge some of your outrage. Also, consider taking up some of the more aggressive sports like boxing, kickboxing, karate, judo, target practice with a really sharp bow. I'm half kidding. Because it works. Canoeing can come later.

Seriously, if you haven't committed to an exercise and nutrition program before, ease into it. Don't make the New Year's Eve resolution mistake of promising yourself to lose twenty pounds and exercise five days a week. You'll fail. And there's nothing worse than throwing guilt about your weight on top of despair about your value. Don't even go there!

During this period of stress and disorientation, it's also important to be hyperaware of what you are and are not eating, how much you're drinking, how many pills you may be taking to sleep or blanket the anxiety, and how much you're moving, getting up from your chair, couch, or the floor to walk—just walk. Start there. It's important to get the blood and oxygen moving so you don't feel inactive and unproductive, physically mirroring the emotional toll of having your work taken away from you.

If you belong to a gym, keep going to the classes or using the machines. Gyms have their own kind of social rituals. They force you to be with people yet minimally interact. This is perfect during this time of avoiding a heart-to-heart, sad-face-emoji conversation.

Recognize that your emotional and physical health are no longer in the margins, between meetings. *You* are the meeting. Don't cancel those meetings. Be accountable to yourself.

CHAPTER THIRTEEN: EMOTIONAL TRIGGERS

The Interview, The Reference Check, and More

While you're on your way to redefining your journey, be prepared: there will be setbacks you hadn't anticipated, including days of anxiety balanced by days of certainty. Even when you think you've mastered the shame of rejection and regained a sense of self bulked up by friends, family, therapists, and business coaches, triggers will come along that throw you back in time or to an emotional place where you don't want to be. It happens. Relax, it's temporary. You're still okay and I'll help you through this by sharing the seven most common triggers that women experienced, so you'll be prepared.

Trigger #1: The employment application

Grace had thought she had repaired enough to inch toward a new job commitment. She agreed to a limited assignment with a major firm as a favor to a friend. She did not anticipate the amount of paperwork that HR would require her to complete or how she would feel explaining her professional history. When she received the employment application, she became paralyzed. It was a standard application requesting her to list her last employers and the reasons for leaving. She didn't know what to say about her most recent employer. She was sure that whatever she said would reveal that she had been asked to leave. For hours, she fiddled with answers:

- To pursue personal goals
- Due to organizational change
- The company had been reorganized
- To pursue new opportunities

But, she thought, *this was* exactly *what people said when they had been let go. I might as well hang a poster board around my neck shouting* "Not Wanted!" She was certain whatever answer she gave would cause her to become an outcast once again. They would see that she had been shunned; that she had done something wrong. She didn't sleep; she twisted in her own blame and misery until a friend said, "What is *wrong* with you? No one actually reads these forms. Just put 'organizational change' and press Send." Grace figured that this answer was closer to the truth: the organization had changed without her. She pressed Send. When she didn't hear back with a thundering condemnation, she had to wonder, *What happened to me? Why am I still so afraid that they'll find out I did something wrong when I didn't?*

Triggers will make your insecurities flare, like a smoldering, chronic illness. You can try to prevent the flares, but chances are they'll take you by surprise. The best way to treat any chronic illness is to acknowledge that it is now a part of your life, and you have to accommodate a new lifestyle to build up tolerance. For Loyalists, this means taking baby steps of risks, like completing an employment application, waiting for the slap on the wrist that never comes, then taking another step. The fear stops as you practice in new circumstances, and the readiness to take the next step becomes stronger.

Trigger #2: The interview question: Why did you leave?

If you left because of a merger, massive layoff, reorganization, or some other economic imperative, this is an easy question to answer. Interviewers understand companies that slash forecasted revenues and need to make tough staffing decisions. You may be thinking, *Why did they choose to lay off me over someone else?* but park that thinking at the door and speak in the corporate tongue that they understand: financials.

It's more difficult if you were suddenly asked to step down, dismissed by a client like Eliza, or asked to be a different person (Patti's experience). One of the women who was interviewed recounted two different reactions to her honest answer: the CEO wanted to take the company in a new direction. In the first case, the HR executive said, "I don't understand. Why did you leave?" When she repeated her answer, he rephrased it for her: "So you're saying he wanted a change of leadership?" He then went on to describe how strong leadership was the single most important quality they were seeking. Of course, she knew that she would not be offered the job and, more importantly, that this was not a cultural fit for her. The second time she tested her answer, the hiring manager who would be her boss said, "It sounds like something else was going on. It happens," and he continued with the interview. And, of course, she knew immediately that she could work with that person.

Remember that sage advice from long ago when you went on many different interviews for jobs? It's still true. You're interviewing them as much as they're interviewing you. If they make you feel like you're hiding something or in any way are less than you are, this is not the place for you. These are not the people for you. As one woman said at the beginning of her journey after being let go, "I realized I should choose my next role based on my boss, *not* the job or the company." Take stock of the qualities and core beliefs that you value and want to be surrounded by each day. Remember, this is your time now, your future by your design.

Trigger #3: The reference check

As Grace got closer to being a finalist for a position, she was asked for references. She thought she had it covered since there were so many colleagues from her former employer who regarded her as a superstar and were shocked to see her let go for reasons that had nothing to do with performance. Grace had a high-caliber list of references. Then the trigger came. The HR person told her, "We have lots of references but we don't have a reference from the person you reported to." Grace stumbled. She did not know what her boss would say. Clearly, this was true, since she did not know the boss would call her in and let her go after she had steadily increased revenues for the year.

Legally, a company can only confirm your employment and provide the dates of your employment. Your boss will likely direct the HR reference checkers to the company's HR division. However, if you're at a senior level, you know your industry is well connected and that information is exchanged "in the vault." Bottom line: if you feel you can't trust what someone will say about you, don't give them as a reference. This is true even if you're reassured by others that bosses don't want to place their companies in jeopardy or place their own judgment in question by giving a poor reference. It is better to move on than to provide an untrustworthy reference. It is important to remember that you want to regain your confidence as you interview and work for a person who believes in *you*, not in what someone else says about you in a reference check, someone whom they don't know.

Here's an interesting twist on this dilemma. I was recently called as a reference for an employee who had been extremely loyal to her company for fifteen years and had finally developed the courage and confidence to take a new, higher-level position at another company. The man who would be her boss asked me, "Why won't she give me her supervisor as a reference?" I told him that they had worked together for fifteen years, and I was sure she wanted to have a job in hand before letting her supervisor know that she would be leaving. They had a very close, loyal relationship. I assured him that there was nothing else to it.

There was no hidden agenda. If you have someone who can say those things for you, and I'm sure you do, give them a heads-up that you haven't given your immediate supervisor as a reference so they can prepare their answer.

Trigger #4: Drinks with former colleagues

You may think you're well on your way to healing and make a date to have drinks with a colleague who is still at the firm that let you go. This is like pressing a cut to see if it will still bleed. You may miss your staff and your recollection of your daily life, which is why you made the date for drinks in the first place. But then you start hearing about how your staff is jockeying for position with the new boss. Intellectually, you realize this is something they must do to survive, but still it hurts if you haven't fully detached from your old company.

Make a promise to yourself: if you want to see your former colleagues, treat it like a desensitizing exercise. Schedule long intervals between each meeting, even months, and be sure to have an activity planned afterward that will lessen the bone-deep sadness you may feel. Even if your reward after your drinks with a former colleague is a phone call with your BFF, schedule the call ahead of time, which also helps to limit your drinking time. Then indulge in your verbal therapy. It may still take time for you to push the sadness and memories away and to pick up where you left off, but that's the nature of desensitizing yourself to *emotional allergens*. Aim for a little exposure at a time to help you cope and build your resilience.

Eventually, you will know that you have built up your immunity when you meet for drinks with a friend who's still with the company, and you're struck by one or more of the following:

- The blandness of continuity
- The problems are the same
- The spin about the problems is the same
- The outlook for the future

- The hype about the outlook for the future
- The amnesia about the past. You may hear the company is finally tackling the challenges you had reported on for the past umpteen years, as if this is novel.

Do you care? No. Not one bit.

Trigger #5: The search firms—all of them

They called you constantly when you were in a position of power. Now you have to call them. This is the nature of the search business. You simply cannot allow your self-esteem to be calibrated according to whether they call you back, give your résumé a fair reading, follow through as they said they would, put you forward just to fill out a "slate," or tell you you're the lead candidate only to call back later with the bad news that the company hired someone else. Their business model is calibrated on making a sale. You know this because you've hired them in the past to recruit for your ex-firm. When you're on the other side of the table as the candidate, waiting for their call, it's easy to forget that they get a percentage of their placement's first-year salary. They have to guarantee the placement will stay one year, and if it doesn't work out, they have to start the search all over again, at no additional cost. You bet they're hustling. Make sure that headhunters are not your only resource for jobs and certainly not a source for reinforcement of your core principles and beliefs about your own worth. Like the HR staff, they work for the company. More often than not, you will land a new role through a connection of your own. As one executive recruiter acknowledged, "In the end it's all about personal connections, and in a good way."

Trigger #6: No one follows you to your new job

You finally land a position that makes you happy and you bubble with excitement, or at least relief. You tell your confidantes from your former job, and they joke that they should leave right now to be with you. You tell them to wait until you assess the current staffing and determine the company's needs, then you'll be back in touch. When you do reach out to your former colleagues, they're suddenly shy, their email server is down, they cancel on check-ins, they become awkward. You realize for the nth time that they are worried about their security, compensation, lifestyles, and perks built up over time given their tenure at the firm. And how can you blame them? "Golden handcuffs"—financial incentives and benefits—are one of the best retention tools for companies. Then there's the fact that what happened to you did not happen to them. You're gone. It's over. Build a new team.

The twist on this trigger: you may find your former staff suddenly available as consultants for your company when things don't work out with the new boss and they need a gig while they search for a new corporate home. If you can, don't hold a grudge—take advantage of this.

Trigger #7: You have a consulting project and worry you're giving away company secrets

The excel sheet format for goals and objectives that you just emailed your client was based on a company-led task force to refine business operations. You have a panic attack that the company will find out and take back all of your severance. Your BFF, who's been fired and rehired more than once, tells you, "Are you kidding? You're not that important anymore."

This cuts to your already porous bones. But you know it's true. You remember the dismantling of other beings before you. Once they were fired or oozed out the door as advisors with less and less time at headquarters, life at the company went on like a merry-go-round. The "new person" was hailed and resourced as a personal buy-in from the top, and all of the focus was on making sure the decision to let you go and hire someone else was the right decision. You are completely forgotten and in the *Who?* zone. Unless you're in possession of trade secrets or CIA-worthy information, the likelihood that someone could construe a shared process as company treason is unlikely. What you're dealing with is an emotional trigger. Harsh but true: you are no longer important to them. Revel in your own peace of mind.

Triggers that fuel our fears, that blow up our anger, that make us cry and deplete our self-esteem, that create and feed guilt, that make us feel like we need to cover up what happened to us—these triggers can come from anywhere: a job application, an interview, a post, a sighting of a former colleague across the street. Expect them. Try to recognize these for what they are: reminders of who we were and the journey we used to be on.

We are not on that journey anymore. This takes time to embrace. It is not that we simply took a detour. We are on a completely different journey, and it will be one of our most life-defining journeys. When your authentic self is able to be expressed outside of the corporate echo chamber, you gain something that very few have the courage *and* opportunity to experience: your own personal power. How often do we have the chance to strike out from where we've been to where we'd like to be? This can be one of the most empowering times of your life.

BEST ADVICE: Desensitizing yourself to emotional triggers takes time, but you will build up immunity and ultimately not remember why you reacted the way you did.

CHAPTER FOURTEEN: RECLAIMING YOUR PERSONAL POWER

Poised for Change

One day it hits you, just like that. You're no longer behaving as your old, fearful, or incensed self.

You're not the person cowering behind a cover-up business card. You're not wondering how to choose your words to explain what happened to you so you don't look like a victim. You're not hiding behind an old reputation and using "Former" as the lead-in to your bio.

Notice how you feel. Pay attention to the signs. Maybe it happens at an interview or a dinner party or as you're reading this book. You suddenly see, really see, through a new lens. You realize that you had been categorizing colleagues on your mental spreadsheet according to your interactions with them related to a particular business transaction or mutual goal or need. Now that you have cultivated these relationships, you see them more holistically, with struggles and triumphs of their own. You had been doing the same fragmented, transactional analysis of your life and career events, the progress measured according to the metrics of your ex-culture and ex-company. Now the dimensions of your prism have changed.

How long this takes to happen cannot be predicted. Whether it happens at all is a question mark. There are so many variables that keep women indignant or in limbo. On the other hand, it may happen more quickly than you think. You may have been poised for change but not quite sure how to do it until the company did it for you.

University of Pennsylvania Professor Martin Seligman, who is known as the father of positive psychology, believes these traumas make us stronger and enable us to better reflect upon and articulate our "life principles." He has researched thousands of individuals, including hundreds of soldiers "who go through a very hard time (and suffer) post-traumatic stress disorder. But a year later they're stronger than they were before by psychological measures." Dr. Seligman calls these traumas a "fork in the road" that forces people to detach from previous goals and ask what else they might do. The critical ingredient for what he calls "post-traumatic growth" is recognizing the new doors that open up to you and being prepared to walk through them.[1] While Dr. Seligman has researched the extreme end of the trauma scale to help men and women who have been in active combat, his belief in the power of positive psychology is applicable to anyone who needs to "grow forward" to reclaim themselves.

BEST ADVICE: You don't have to have all of the answers to know it's time to choose a different path.

PART FIVE

Your Brave
New World

CHAPTER FIFTEEN: BEGINNING AGAIN

Stories of Resilience

Let's review the stages of bereavement devised by John Bowlby and Colin Murray Parkes that I've used throughout this book. To refresh our memories, they are:

- **Stage 1**: Shock and Numbness—see Part One
- **Stage 2**: Yearning and Searching—see Part Two
- **Stage 3**: Disorientation and Disorganization—see Parts Three and Four
- **Stage 4**: Reorganization and Resolution—where we are now, Part Five

Of Stage Four, the researchers write: "During this stage [your child] begins to accept the loss and assimilate it into her life. In addition . . . to seeming less sad, she has more energy and is able to think clearly again."[1]

This is where you begin again. You know you've made it to Stage Four when:

- Ninety percent of your conversation no longer concerns what happened to you in the past but what is happening now.
- You've stopped calling people from your old company for "news."
- You have a new group of relationships, and they know little about your former tormented self.
- Your work–life balance is better than it's ever been.
- You've been able to stick to your health and exercise routine for at least one month.
- You look in the mirror and see that the worry lines are gone. A huge burden has been lifted, and it shows.
- Something major has happened in your life that you always dreamed about but never had time to think about.
- You like yourself. You really do.

We know that life is messy, so you've probably assumed that the stages of bereavement are not as linear as they appear. You're right. They bleed into each other, and as I've said, some women can hop forward to one and back to another, then leap to Stage Four. The most important and wonderful realization is the way you feel when you are no longer in the stages of yearning and mourning. Listen to these seven stories of women who successfully achieved the fourth stage of resolution and have rediscovered their happiness and themselves.

Allison's story: "Leaving was the most empowering thing I ever did."

Allison worked for a Broadway production company for more than twenty-two years. During that time, the company changed from a family-owned business to a multimillion-dollar enterprise, and she rose from being the manager of budgets and staffing to become the chief operating officer. She had a close relationship with the founders who were known for taking risks that paid off in blockbusters. The entrepreneurial, independent, yet intimate culture made her one of the company's strongest advocates and Loyalists. Her days were exciting and focused on keeping the company profitable while helping to build a collaborative, trusting, and intensely creative culture.

During the last five years of Allison's tenure, the founding member of the production company announced that he was stepping back from the day-to-day management of the company. After the requisite search, the board approved a new CEO to replace him. This is when Allison's faux-firing began. Almost immediately, the CEO set about implementing changes to bring more corporate rigor to the company, something Allison knew was one of the board's goals. However, in the process, the company's culture struggled with its identity. It was changing from a family business known for its quirky successes to a corporate-driven, Hollywood-type studio. Allison became the lightning rod for complaints from disgruntled staff and directives from the CEO to "fix the culture."

Being the Loyalist she was, Allison *did* try to fix it. She brought in consultants to conduct a culture assessment, and the conclusion, Allison said, "was that the culture was in the tank and suffering from a lack of trust."

The CEO rejected the results. "This was a pivotal moment for me," Allison said. "I knew it was time for me to go."

Allison realized that she would need help leaving since she was still tied to the image of the company she had helped build and to the people who had been a part of her life for more than two decades. Allison reached out to a group of close friends, and they made a pact to put the day she would resign on all their calendars. They even had a secret code: Halcyon Day. "I needed a group of people who would hold me to it," she said. Allison's self-awareness of her vulnerability is a good lesson, and her solution is worth remembering.

The morning she had planned to resign in a face-to-face meeting came with the news that the CEO would not be in the office. Allison felt that, if she waited, she would compromise her commitment to herself. She practiced some meditation, rehearsed in her mind what she would say, then picked up the phone and called the CEO. The effect on Allison was immediate: an explosion of jubilation and relief.

"The minute I told her I quit and hung up the phone, I thought, *Why didn't I tell her that five years ago?* Five years ago! It was the most empowering thing I ever did. The fear was gone. I was really scared before I quit about how I was going to pay my bills. I was afraid of not having a daily rhythm, stability, consistency, a paycheck. But from that day forward, I was never afraid. The fear of the unknown before I left was actually worse than when I was *in* the unknown!"

Allison did a life-changing maneuver: she took control back. She was in control of her fears and emotions, which allowed her to reframe the moment.

Again, did all of this happen instantaneously, and voilà, a new Allison emerged? Absolutely not! It took an investment in herself through many different pathways, and it took time.

BEST ADVICE: Imagine you just filed Chapter 11 on your life and need to emerge as a new entity.

Allison had many projects at home that had been neglected for years. Did she spring into action as if nothing had happened? No, she did not. She went to sleep. She slept for days, physically and emotionally exhausted. Then she began traveling and volunteering for organizations that needed her expertise. "I did a lot of soul-searching and journalizing and visualizing where I wanted to be. I enrolled in a class in art history, I studied languages, I studied topics that had been outside of my previous experiences." This was very different from the Allison who had worked 24-7 for twenty-two years, always putting her job ahead of her life and personal development.

"When I was with the company, I thought, *I need a paycheck. I can never be a consultant.*" Now she was asking herself, *Who do I want to be instead of the safe person bringing home a paycheck?*

To help herself move on, Allison made extensive use of a vision board. "I created one on my computer. I asked myself, *What kind of environment do I want to work in? How do I want to feel? What kind of people do I want to be with?* I printed out my vision board and put it in a beautiful silver frame on my desk. It helped me a lot. I'd spend a lot of time studying it when I was on the phone or working at my desk, and it reminded me of the things that I loved and where I wanted to be. I've never updated it. It's still true."

Today, Allison is working full time with one of the organizations for which she previously consulted. She has helped create and distribute for theaters around the world a number of productions about the struggles and achievements of undocumented children and families. "It's a dream come true," she said. "I wanted to be closer to the programming and creative side of the business and not stuck in operations. I'm also considering a degree in international development."

Allison had tried for more than five years to "fix a culture," partner with a CEO whose management style was very different from her own, quell the fears and disruptions of the staff, and keep a company profitable while grieving for the story of what the company had been. She spoke endlessly of leaving but would return each morning to try again, ultimately falling ill, which her medical team traced back to her stress. Her body was sending her a message to override the deep fear and pain of moving on. Today, Allison says with confidence, "Anticipation is so much worse than the action. The fear of the unknown is much greater than anything you will encounter."

ALLISON'S BEST ADVICE: "Don't sell yourself short. You'll find another way to contribute. Move on. Listen to your intuition and listen to your gut. My position now feels really natural and comfortable. You'll know it when you find it."

For those of us used to the structure, analyses, case studies, culture of deliverables, hierarchical organizations, and all of the scaffolding that holds up the world of business: "knowing it when you find it" is a foggy, alien concept with hardly the strength of a feather to hold it up. Yet, last year alone at least fifty books were published about happiness, and none of them talk about finding it in a staff meeting.

Ellen Kullman's story: A portfolio for a new life

Ellen Kullman, who had a long, successful career as the CEO of Dupont, spoke to Veronica Dagher of the *Wall Street Journal* in the podcast *Secrets of Wealthy Women* about what it's like when there is a sudden career change . . . when Ellen was no longer the CEO. "First of all, it's very disconcerting because you wake up one day and all of a sudden you don't have anything to do. And I got a lot of advice from a lot of people who reached out to me, and the common advice they gave me was, 'Don't take anything on for six months.' And it's the right piece of advice. But it is really hard to do. Because the first couple of months, that's easy, you can enjoy yourself, take a vacation, spend time with the kids; then the kids get worried you're going to put all your attention on them and they want you to get busy. And then the phone's ringing a lot in those first couple of months, and you're saying, 'no, no, no.' Then the phone stops ringing because you told them, you know, don't call me until six months are up. Then you start worrying. 'Maybe I'm not relevant anymore. What should I be doing?' But then all of a sudden, the phone starts ringing again. And you've had time to reflect on whether you want another full-time position, or do you want a portfolio? I realized that I hadn't had any flexibility in my life for thirty-five years, and that flexibility was really a lot of fun—to put together different things that I was passionate about, to spend time with my family and friends, to give back. So I chose to put together a portfolio."[2]

ELLEN KULLMAN'S BEST ADVICE: Take the opportunity to create a portfolio of your passions as the next chapter of your life's work.

Jenny's story: Making a life-changing commitment

"About nine months after I was let go [from the publishing company], a friend persuaded me to go to her retirement party. I didn't think my former boss [who had let her go] would be there, since he never attended those kinds of events. He was. When he saw me, he stood up and gave me a hug. All I could think was that I felt pretty good. His life hadn't changed. But mine had. He hadn't gone through the growth process I had put myself through, and there was an entire world outside of that company. I went home feeling that I had successfully stepped off the hamster wheel."

As part of her growth process with the outplacement agency, Jenny accepted a volunteer role with a cause that was meaningful to her, lung disease. She volunteered every week in the local hospital. Through this commitment, she met the woman who became her new boss at a health care organization. Jenny made her decision based on the culture of the organization, which was very different from the one she had devoted her life to for twenty-three years. She was thrilled by the opportunity to provide her years of experience to a brave new world. "When I told the hospital that I could no longer volunteer because I was starting a full-time job, they honored me with an award for my commitment. It was life-changing. And none of this would have happened if I had stayed where I was and not gone through this process."

JENNY'S BEST ADVICE: "If you do the hard work of figuring out what you want to do next and who you want to be and sign on to do it honestly, you will only benefit. There is only an upside. No downside."

Grace's story: Reframing success

Grace was walking home from a networking event where she had seen scores of people in the business that she had known for decades, including her colleagues and staff from her former firm. Suddenly it struck her. She had changed. She was no longer seeing her network as her old self but as her new self through a different lens. She recognized the courage and grit of all the women who had ventured out on their own and had been running their businesses for a long time. When she was a hiring manager, she thought of them as consultants chasing after clients and worrying about getting paid. But no. They were independent contractors—emphasis on *independent*. They were entrepreneurial thinkers and business people who recast their lives as they wanted them to be. They figured this out, some decades ago. Grace now took stock of how they marketed themselves, how they poured their passion into their work, how they built a business around their own brand, their own lives.

Grace went on to have different, more authentic relationships with her former colleagues and others she had known for years because she had entirely different interactions with them. She valued them for what they had accomplished rather than for what they could do for Grace. As a result, new opportunities and new people came into her life that were more varied and exciting than she had experienced in decades. Grace found herself enjoying a state of being she hadn't inhabited since childhood when she had moments of pure laughter and excitement, rather than apprehension about the path forward. Her jaw no longer cracked, her teeth weren't grinding, and her stomach wasn't knotty. She realized how happy she was by knowing how unhappy she had been.

The clearest sense of how far she had traveled dawned on Grace during a mentoring session with a young woman who claimed to be at a crossroads in her career. Grace told the young woman to flip a coin and was rewarded with an incredulous stare. "Trust me," she said. The coin showed heads and the woman looked unhappy. "What matters is your reaction," Grace explained to her. "How do you feel? Are you happy or disappointed?" To Grace, it really was that simple. Happiness was the real "get."

Lidia's story: Proud of her new life

Lidia had suffered both as a compliance executive and as a Loyalist who was let go from a job she loved. She was asked by her bosses to fire people she valued and was then fired herself for knowing too much. She admits that the signs were all obvious that she needed to detach from the company, but she chose to ignore what she saw. Lidia was the source of financial support for her family, and not once did she give up hope that she would find another position. She used her faith to shore up her resilience and persistence. She also reached out to a therapist and professional coach. It took her eighteen months to find a new role and another seven years to achieve a vice presidency at her new company. But she did it! Along the way, she learned and practiced how to be emotionally detached from her job. She became an expert at helping employees without becoming personally involved in their lives: providing references for counseling rather than counseling them herself, leaving at the end of the day rather than de-stressing with gossip and company news, keeping her own opinions and sentiments to herself. It was difficult but, as she said, "I'll never make myself that vulnerable again." Instead, she now feels "beyond strong. My faith is beyond strong."

"At this point in my life," Lidia said, "there is so much less stress. It is so much better. My interactions with staff and my boss are strictly business. They have no idea what I really think and what I really feel. I'm even better now at doing my job because I'm focused on being judged for my work, on the final product, not on my relationships with people. I have a reputation at this new company as someone people can trust, as someone with integrity. It means a lot to me that my department is a place people can trust, especially after what I went through."

LIDIA'S BEST ADVICE: "When you're in a position of managing people, remember they're not your friends. Be good to them but don't cross the line. There's more strength and freedom in being detached."

Laura's story: Living her passions every day

After Laura left the attorney general's office for a career in fundraising, she had a number of positions at nonprofit hospitals and universities. At a university in New York City, she completed one of their most successful fundraising campaigns and was proud of her record-breaking accomplishment. Nevertheless, the university appointed a new president who brought his own chief fundraising professional with him, and Laura was once again out of a job. That was a life-altering moment for her.

Laura laughs now. "When this happened to me, my partner said, 'You're going to get younger.' And she was right. The worry lines disappeared. I de-aged." Laura realized that her heart really wasn't in proving herself at another high-pressure job and that she needed to take time to examine her passions and where they could lead.

Laura became excited by the prospect of solving a problem she had seen demonstrated repeatedly in the fundraising field: people's inability to ask for money. "Let's face it," she said, "if you can't ask for money when your profession was established to ask for money, there's a problem." Laura wanted to create a firm devoted to teaching people not only how to ask for money but to ask for whatever they needed: a raise, a new house, a divorce, a new contract, anything in business and life. Laura approached herself as if she were a new company, recruiting people who could advise and guide her in her new venture, including a branding consultant, producer, financial counselor, and more. "Unfortunately," she said, "people often don't think enough of themselves to invest in themselves. I don't believe in that." Laura had setbacks, certainly, and made mistakes, but her passion kept her going, and her knowledge that she did not want to go back "inside the system" kept her facing forward.

LAURA'S BEST ADVICE: "Figure out the fear. It's cathartic to determine why you might be the right person for something entirely new."

Today, Laura is the founder and CEO of The Ask. She is the best-selling author of five books and has spoken to audiences around the world. She's appeared on ABC news with Katie Couric, given tips to Anderson Cooper, and been featured in the *Wall Street Journal* and the *Huffington Post*, among other sites. She was recently honored with New York Nonprofit Network's "50 over 50 Award for excellence in media and philanthropy." Is she wealthy? No. Does she have to chase new business constantly? Yes. Is she miserable? Far from it. She is ecstatic, living her passions every day.

Almost all of us will need help because moving forward is not a straightforward one-two-three process. It's more like a one to zero to negative-five to three process. As long as you have your goal clearly stated, even if it's something as personal as "I never want to be hurt like that again," you can get there, or at least, you can get away from where you've been.

You can get help from therapists, business coaches, outplacement firms, friends, family, colleagues. You can practice meditation, exercise therapy, spa therapy, and rapid transformation therapy. You can explore spiritual guidance, vision boards, adventure tours—anything and everything that allows you to think about and experience yourself in a new way will help you. I'm sure there are limitless experiences for which you never had time before that will enable you to grow new perceptions of yourself. The journey doesn't have to be radical, though it can be. It just has to be a deliberate, ongoing focus on reframing your thoughts about yourself and the uncertainties you face.

In *Getting Things Done: The Art of Stress-Free Productivity*, David Allen talks about the need to get everything out of our heads into an organized system so that we're not constantly thinking about what we have to do. The mind just goes in circuits, he says, it can't really execute.[3]

The same holds true for the negative thoughts and "shoulda woulda couldas." If you don't get them out of your head into some kind of holding pen, they will become the major organizing force for your thoughts and perceptions. You can't see what's in front of you with a swarm of predators circling your heart and soul.

Now there were women who were interviewed for this book whose stories were not included. Those were heartbreaking interviews filled with rage about firings that happened many, many years ago. They had not allowed themselves to evolve. Some of them were even mentoring women to hold on to their bitterness as a power tool.

But out of all those interviewed, 80 percent did recast their lives by embracing uncertainty, not as a threat but as a necessity. They learned to relax in the unstructured world of possibilities. They all worked very hard at changing the scripts in their minds, using new words when talking to themselves and disciplining themselves to be detached from external judgments both good and bad, not always successfully but enough to overcome paralysis. They chose to reflect, to give themselves time to rediscover their passions and projects, and to become spiritual daredevils exploring long-ago root problems that may have led to the choices they made.

Shushan Aleaqui, business and transformational coach, believes in Einstein's premise that "the same mind that created the problem can't be used to come up with the solution." She has guided hundreds of women to understand the root causes of their choices so that they can begin to change the way they see their future paths.

My story: Empowering others

Similar to the women I interviewed, after I left my organization, I read a lot of books, journaled, had the help of various coaches, learned from their stories, went on a lot of bad dates with potential employers, had my share of bombshell interviews, took two steps forward and three steps back, and walked into the best opportunity of my life that came to me at the right time from someone I hadn't spoken to in years. It was a "Deepak moment." I had stopped forcing solutions, which had always been my Achilles heel, and let the right people and opportunities materialize. I worked hard on recognizing these opportunities, "deglazing" my biases so that I could see people as more than a product of their professions—and even more importantly, so that I could see myself in their worlds, which were far removed in some cases from my previous life. I did not engage in a typical broadband networking campaign. I was selective about the connections I made, using only a few criteria:

- Will this be an interesting meeting?
- Will I learn something new?
- Will I be able to help this person in any way?
- Will they be able to help me in any way?
- Will this help me decide on my next step?

As I mentioned, if I came away with just one new idea or action step, I felt the meeting had been a success.

My criteria led me down alleys and up boulevards, with real spikes of happiness when I came away with new knowledge. In many of John Maxwell's leadership books, he encourages us to talk with those we admire about their lives and their choices, not so much about the things they accomplished. For me, this was like going to school for free, and better yet, it was a school where you learned what really happened behind the scenes in people's lives, not just what the textbooks codified. During my journey, I met with a billionaire environmentalist, a finance guru who was also a degreed philosopher, CEOs who had lost their jobs and reinvented themselves, the leader of a billion-dollar educational system, a pioneer in New York state government, a real estate multimillionaire, faculty from a prestigious Ivy League business school, representatives from an internationally renowned scientific research institute, board members from a social service agency, and of course all the women interviewed for this book. We talked about their lives, choices, aspirations, and frustrations. The commonality of the human spirit, unfiltered, was striking. Did all of this have a direct connection to a job? No. Did all of this open up worlds of possibilities about how others conducted their lives? Yes. Did this help me define what was most important to me in my search? Yes. Did it help me determine what I was looking for in a leader and how to be a better leader? Yes. Did it give me a sense of the variety of organizational cultures that existed so I could figure out what was best for me? Yes.

When the people I met with asked me what I was looking to do next, I had a pat answer: "I want to use all my leadership experience and fund-raising skills to help an organization that really needs it." It was so pat, crisp, and user-friendly, I barely heard it anymore. Until I realized it was true!

While I was being considered for leadership positions in three prestigious organizations, I found myself drawn to a smaller organization that had enormous potential and was newly helmed by one of the most genuine leaders I had ever met. As soon as we began talking, I knew she was the right person coming into my life at the right time. The icing on the cake: the organization's mission was focused on social justice issues. This was like returning home for me. I didn't realize exactly what had been missing from my heart until I stepped into the room with this leader and heard her story, her history, and her goals.

Could I have ever imagined this existence inside the culture I had left? No. Is it possible that this urge was always buried deep inside? Yes. Have I developed new dreams? You bet.

As I met with many women on my journey, I realized that I had seen too many of us who were unaware of our talents and potential. I had done my best to sponsor these women, not just mentor them, but to set them up for success using my influence. Still, I had a gnawing sense that I could do more and that the system of beliefs and techniques that I used to propel my colleagues and staff forward would be helpful to a larger audience of women. I was concerned about women rising in the business world with the same questions, concerns, fears, and limiting beliefs that no one would suspect they carried under their strong professional personas. While getting fired is the chau gong of wake-up alarms, there are more symphonic passages to self-actualization, and I wanted to help more women be their own orchestra conductor.

My driving mission is to give women the strength to rediscover their own voice, hold on to their personal power, and reclaim their future. My approach is based on six values that form the heart and soul of this book. I give them to you now as the product of my journey and hopefully as inspiration for yours.

- **Respect Your Innovative Mindset:** Before anyone told you how to think, you connected the dots on your own and drew your own conclusions. Celebrate your beliefs and *carry the voice of empowerment.*

- **Carry the Voice of Empowerment:** Use it to empower yourself and pass it on, because everyone needs to be reminded of their value. You can always use a little light to help *reframe your moments.*

- **Reframe Your Moments:** You define what your life means to you—appreciate the bad for all of its good. Don't take everything at face value; don't be afraid to change your mind, stop, and *tune into your energy.*

- **Tune into Your Energy:** Life can be challenging, and life can be confusing. Be attentive to how you feel, not only what you think, and it will help you make choices and *fear less.*

- **Fear Less:** Fear stops us from moving forward. It's a script we repeat to ourselves and one of the toughest habits to break. The absence of fear brings surprising freedom, even when we *face the unknown.*

- **Face the Unknown:** Moving ahead means traveling through uncertainty—and that's necessary. You'll be transformed by the journey in ways you could never imagine.

CHAPTER SIXTEEN: STAYING COURAGEOUS

Sustaining Your Success

So we've gone through this existential evolution together, from the actual moment of being fired, to the internalization of what happened, to the get-up-off-the-floor-and-do-something moments, and all the way to realizing you have been changed for the better. Thank you for staying with me.

I'd like to leave you with one last tool that has helped me gain perspective and strength throughout many unpredictable, mystifying, or hurtful situations. Quotable quotes are something I carry with me on the backs of envelopes, in book underlinings, and in my memory. They're the words I need when I can't find my own, to paraphrase a classic line from *Finding Forrester*. They can change my attitude, mood, and outlook and give me courage or a tension-breaking laugh when I desperately need it. Here are a number of phrases extracted from the book or straight from the back of my envelopes for your easy reference to keep you moving forward with determination:

- You must believe that what happened to you *had* to happen so you could move forward professionally and personally.

- Your ego is keeping you unhappy since it thrives on the junk food of title, position, and power.
- There is no vaccination against dysfunction. Be vigilant about the stress around you and the people you trust.
- You can't see what's in front of you with a swarm of predators circling your heart and soul.
- You may have been poised for change but not quite sure how to do it until the company did it for you.
- Resilience requires a pact with yourself. When you make a pact to reflect on what really works best for you, no matter what anyone else says, you build core psychological strength that makes you more resilient.
- Embrace uncertainty not as a threat but as a necessity.
- Learn how to relax in the unstructured world of possibilities.
- Reframe your fear of the unknown as the joy of surprise and opportunity.
- Trust that the right people will enter your life when you need them.
- Don't confuse moving quickly with moving forward.
- Anticipating the unknown is much worse than the unknown itself.
- What happened to you is a gift.
- The commonality of the human spirit, unfiltered, is striking and uplifting.
- The best part of your journey are the people you never knew existed who come to your aid.

One Last Word: A Bonus You Didn't Count On

At least once in your life, someone has called you a role model, right? Your daughter, other daughters, young women on your staff? You would hear this and be somewhat surprised—after all, you were just being you—or the opposite, you were in fact über aware, after down-and-dirty struggles, that you had illuminated a path that they could now follow.

Guess what? You've just done it again.

You have become a living, breathing demonstration of what really happens when women get fired and how they cope and build resilience. Other women will be attracted to your energy. "Hey," said a high-powered COO who had watched her C-suite colleagues be knocked out of the box, "it could happen at any time to any one of us. That's the nature of business." Exactly. And when the tornado tears down your ego, you've got to rebuild, this time with stronger materials.

What happened to you needed to happen to open up a larger world of opportunity for you. Shushan Aleaqui calls it "the blessing of being fired." You may think that's going too far, especially if you're at Stage One: "Shock and Numbness." But at Stage Four: "Reorganization and Resolution," you see things a little differently. Okay, so you, the straight-A role model, flunked a semester. Now you're going to a new college you never even knew existed before. By taking care of yourself, you're in a better position to take care of others. You put your oxygen mask on first. As Grace's daughter said to her a year after Grace had been fired and reframed her life, "You seem happier. You're more present."

Grace felt it herself. She texted her BFF, "I find myself increasingly happy each day." Her BFF gave her a thumbs-up back, texting, "You must know what you want in your life and finally moved beyond the company." Grace texted back, "Yes I do know what I want in my life now." She chalked it up to only one thing: the joy of being fired.

The End—a.k.a. The Beginning

EPILOGUE

"I hadn't seen my boss face-to-face since March," Alana tells me. "For months we had been in conversations about which staff we were going to furlough and how we were going to operate without them. In those months I kept thinking about how this was going to look to our clients. Little did I know I was being discussed without my knowledge."

It's January 2021, and I'm on the phone with Alana who was let go during the pandemic. Like so many others who were fired in every other year, she was given no warning. It came as a surprise. In fact, she knew when the meetings were happening to make the final decisions about her staff; she just didn't know that she was on the agenda.

"One morning I got an email from my boss telling me that he was going to be in town. He asked if we could get together at a cafe we both knew. I was wondering how I'd feel when I saw him because it had been over six months. I was the first one there wearing a face mask at a table outside, and who's standing there but the HR person. I walked over and said, 'Oh, it's that meeting.' Then my boss came."

Alana stops talking and I can imagine her reliving the scene in her mind when she was both managing and crumbling. "You never know how you're going to act in that moment," she continues. "It's a lot to take in when it's happening. I kept thinking, *I'm not going to give it to them. If I fall apart, it's going to be in a private way.* For maybe half a second, the HR person went to grab a tissue for me, and I said, 'No I'm fine.' I wasn't going to give it to them." She repeats this several times. "What was *it*?" I ask. "The emotion. I felt like I owned that. I did not want them to see me break down. My reputation is everything to me. I wanted to walk out the way I walked in. I had been successful. The numbers didn't lie. I felt the unfairness of it. But I wasn't going to let it define who I was. I didn't want to give them defeat."

Alana's strength didn't suddenly erupt. It had been building over years of political chess games where her performance was legendary but the leadership machinations were fierce. She had practice resisting defeat, and this strengthened her resolve. She tells me, "I kept thinking that I wish my boss had gotten to know who I am at my core. My moral strength."

She pauses. "After a week or so, I realized something. The pandemic was actually making this process easier. I was working from home like everyone else, so I wasn't in the public eye. I had cover. No one could say, 'Why isn't she on the train today? Did you see her come home from work?' No one knew anything. I wasn't missing out on the office meetings and get-togethers. *Everyone* was isolated."

She continues, warming to the memory of how she handled herself. "I became very strategic. I took time to myself. I started telling people my story when I was ready to tell them and I only told people who could help me." (In other words, she didn't add drama to her trauma.) "Sure there were a few duds, like the ones who gasped and said, 'Didn't you see this coming?' Why would someone ask me that?" She pauses, incredulous. "Because they want to know if they should be watching for signs," I say.

She didn't have to walk the plank down the halls of the office. No one was there. She did go in to collect her belongings, but because of COVID-19, there wasn't much she hadn't already taken home. Except her shoes. She had to empty her shoe drawer. How many of us have one of those? How many of us have even looked at a stiletto since the pandemic?

She didn't have to go to the dreaded cocktail parties and professional meetings, and make up scripts about what she was doing and planning and why she didn't have a business card. "I did run into one person at the grocery store who asked me what I was doing. I said I was in between *things*." She laughs.

These silver linings are real during this pandemic when employment opportunities are bleak. But any amount of diminished suffering and pain is an amount I'll take gladly.

What small slivers of comfort can we gain from being outside of the work norm when we're let go? Megan Marzo, the behavioral therapist who opened this book with her observations about coping, believes that many times the stories we tell ourselves about events are outdated, untrue, or not working for us in a changed world.

This was the case for Alana. After strategically weighing three paths forward, after interviewing people who were happy or unhappy with their choices, she chose her future. She was not going back into the corporate machine she'd known for thirty years, but striking out on her own as an entrepreneur. In fact, she had put in a competitive bid for her first project and she got it. She was full of wonder. "I can't tell you how many people were helpful; how many people were so generous with their time and connections." Her first job came from a friend. "It's amazing," she continues, "how these things just show up when you need them." Just as I've been saying all along.

Alana and I talked for a long time, until she had to hang up because the next day was her first day with her new client. In spite of the dire circumstances in which we still find ourselves, she and I ended on an upbeat note. We'd been through the firings, been wrung out by bosses, been depleted by companies, become entrepreneurial during the greatest economic disaster since the Great Depression, and yet we were happy. Tough hides for tough times. May your own force be with you.

January 2021

APPENDIX

Music to Evolve By

Playlists for Each Phase of Your Journey

Do you remember when you used to "go to your room" to listen to music when you had those moody days or confusing nights or wanted to celebrate something special in private? Let's recreate that secret chamber. These suggested playlists will help you vent in the privacy of your home, validate your feelings, give you hope that all is not lost, and inspire you to revel in your own victories.

Part One: The Loyalists' Guide to Betrayal

"New Rules," Dua Lipa
"Run," Nicole Scherzinger
"Narcissus," Alanis Morissette
"Hearts a Mess," Gotye

Part Two: Being Faux-Fired and Other Involuntary Departures

"Cruel Summer," Bananarama
"Don't Come Around Here No More," Tom Petty & The Heartbreakers

"Nobody Seems To Care," 16 Bit Lolitas
"Work B**ch," Britney Spears

Part Three: Leaning Out: Going Public, One Surprise at a Time

"Galvanize," The Chemical Brothers
"Keep Holding On," Avril Lavigne
"Don't Give Up," Chicane, Bryan Adams
"The Right Life," Seal

Part Four: Preparing for Your Next Role

"No Tears Left to Cry," Ariana Grande
"All or Nothing," Dirty Vegas
"I Won't Back Down," Tom Petty & The Heartbreakers
"Broken Glass," Rachel Platten
"Light Me Up," The Pretty Reckless
"Good Feeling," Flo Rida

Part Five: Your Brave New World

"Can't Hold Us," Macklemore and Ryan Lewis
"I Can See Clearly Now," Jimmy Cliff
"Newborn Friend," Seal
"Confident," Demi Lovato
"I'm So Excited," Pointer Sisters
"Keep This Party Going," The B-52s
"Firework," Katy Perry
"I Will Survive," Gloria Gaynor

ENDNOTES

Preface

1. Julie Creswell, "Mass Firing on Zoom is Latest Sign of Weight Watchers Unrest," *New York Times*, May 22, 2020, www.nytimes.com /2020/05/22/business/weight-watchers-firings-zoom.html.

Introduction: The Day the Earth Stands Still

1. Brené Brown, *Dare to Lead* (New York: Random House, 2018).

Chapter One: You Were Fired. Now What?

1. Jennifer Wolf, "Four Stages of Grief in Children," 2018, www .liveabout.com/the-stages-of-grief-in-children-2997220.

2. Nicki Lisa Cole, "Goffman's Front Stage and Back Stage Behavior," 2018, www.thoughtco.com/goffmans-front-stage-and-back-stage -behavior-4087971.

3. Robert Hogan, "Reflections on the Dark Side," 2015, http://info .hoganassessments.com.

4. Michael Weishan, "A Woman Is Like a Tea Bag: Eleanor Roosevelt, and Radical Women of the 20s and 30s 3-26," 2018, www.fdr foundation/eleanor-too-radical-women-of-the-1920s-and-1930s.

Chapter Two: The Next Twelve Hours

1. Eleanor Roosevelt, *You Learn by Living: Eleven Keys for a More Fulfilling Life* (New York: HarperCollins Publisher, 2011).

Chapter Three: The Morning's Wake-Up Call

1. www.dictionary.com/browse/rites-of-passage.

2. Annamarie Mann, "Why We Need Best Friends at Work," 2018, www.gallup.com/workplace/236213/why-need-best-friends -work.aspx.

3. Erin Griffith, "Why Are Young People Pretending to Love Work?" *New York Times*, January 26, 2019, www.nytimes.com/2019/01/26 /business/against-hustle-culture-rise-and-grind-tgim.html.

4. Erin Griffith, "Why Are Young People Pretending to Love Work?" *New York Times*, January 26, 2019, www.nytimes.com/2019/01/26 /business/against-hustle-culture-rise-and-grind-tgim.html.

5. Kristin Wong, "How to Detach Emotionally from Work," 2017, www.thecut.com/2017/11/how-to-emotionally-detach-from -work.html.

Chapter Four: Tech Hell

1. "The Number of Email Addresses People Use," 2018, www.zetta sphere.com/how-many-email-addresses-people-typically-use/.

2. Ama and Stephanie Marston, *Type R: Transformative Resilience for Thriving in a Turbulent World* (New York: Hatchett Book Group, 2018).

3. www.goodreads.com/quotes/9479-it-s-the-friends-you-can-call-up-at-4-a-m.

Chapter Six: Getting Faux-Fired

1. Greg Smith, "Why I Am Leaving Goldman Sachs," *New York Times*, March 14, 2012, www.nytimes.com/2012/03/14/opinion/why-i-am-leaving-goldman-sachs.html.

2. Adam Bryant, "How to Be a CEO, From a Decade's Worth of Them," *New York Times*, October 27, 2017, www.nytimes.com/2017/10/27/business/how-to-be-a-ceo.html.

Chapter Seven: You Are Not Alone, a.k.a. This Happens More Than You Think

1. "Women CEOs of the S&P 500," *Catalyst*, 2017, www.catalyst.org/research/women-ceos-of-the-sp-500/.

2. Emma Hinchliffe, "CEO Turnover Reached an All-Time High in August," *Fortune*, September 12, 2018, https://fortune.com/2018/09/12/ceo-turnover-record-high.

3. Alice Walton, "Female CEOs Are More Likely to Be Fired than Males, Study Finds," *Forbes*, December 1, 2018, www.forbes.com/sites/alicegwalton/2018/12/01/female-ceos-are-more-likely-to-be-fired-than-males-study-finds.

4. Ama and Stephanie Marston, *Type R: Transformative Resilience for Thriving in a Turbulent World* (New York Hatchett Book Group, 2018).

Chapter Eight: Telling Staff, Family, and Friends

1. Mika Brzezinski, *Knowing Your Value: Women, Money, and Getting What You're Worth* (New York: Weinstein Books, 2011).

Chapter Nine: On Your Mark, Get Ready, Network!

1. Minda Zetlin, "How to Network Like You Really Mean It," *Inc.*, March 28, 2014, www.inc.com/minda-zetlin/8-things-power -networkers-do-make-connections.html.

Chapter Eleven: Embracing Uncertainty

1. Ellen Langer, *Counterclockwise: Mindful Health and the Power of Possibility* (New York: Ballentine Books, 2009).

2. Deepak Chopra, *The Seven Spiritual Laws of Success* (San Rafael, CA: Amber-Allen Publishing and New World Library, 1994), 56.

3. Mark Nepo, *The Book of Awakening* (San Francisco: Conari Press, 2011), 10.

4. Ama and Stephanie Marston, *Type R: Transformative Resilience for Thriving in a Turbulent World* (New York: Hatchett Book Group, 2018), 26.

5. Mark Nepo, *The Book of Awakening* (San Francisco: Conari Press, 2011), 10.

6. "Stockholm syndrome," Wikipedia, https://en.wikipedia.org/wiki /Stockholm_syndrome.

7. Jenny Blake, *Pivot* (New York: Penguin Random House, 2016), 11.

8. Genesis Advisors, *Harvard Business Review*, and International Institute of Management Development, 2011, unpublished electronic survey.

9. Jim Collins, *Good to Great*, October 2001, retrieved from www.jimcollins.com.

10. Deepak Chopra, *The Seven Spiritual Laws of Success* (San Rafael, CA: Amber-Allen Publishing and New World Library, 1994), 57.

11. Carlos Castaneda, *The Art of Dreaming*, 1993, retrieved from www.federaljack.com.

12. Joel Comm, "3 Reasons Why Flying First Class Is Worth Every Penny," *Inc.*, February 26, 2016, www.inc.com/joel-comm/3-reasons-flying-first-class-is-worth-every-penny.html.

Chapter Twelve: Affirming Yourself

1. Richard N. Bolles, *What Color Is Your Parachute?* (New York: Ten Speed Press, 2019).

Chapter Fourteen: Reclaiming Your Personal Power

1. Sara Green Carmichael, "On Mental Toughness," interview by Martin Seligman, *Harvard Business Review*, March 2011.

Chapter Fifteen: Beginning Again

1. Jennifer Wolf, "Four Stages of Grief in Children," 2018, www.liveabout.com/the-stages-of-grief-in-children-2997220.

2. "Former Dupont CEO Ellen Kullman: Changing Culture Key," interview by Veronica Dagher, *Wall Street Journal* podcast *Secrets*

of Wealthy Women, July 31, 2018, www.wsj.com/podcasts/secrets
-of-wealthy-women.

3. David Allen, *Getting Things Done: The Art of Stress-Free Productivity*
(New York: Penguin Books, 2015), Part 1.

ACKNOWLEDGMENTS

I have so much gratitude for the many people who helped bring this book to life. Thank you to my BFF Joan Lewis for your unwavering support and point-of-view that has always made me see the truth behind the curtain. Thank you to the many friends, colleagues, and women who spoke to me over wine, coffee, and tea, whispering their pain and sharing their rediscovered joy in both the dark and light corners of our worlds. Thank you to Laura Fredricks, Bob Cooper, Jenny Friedman, Dominic Ianno, Lisa Marie Vasquez, Judy Bass, Megan Marzo, and Barrett Briske. And just because . . . thank you to the late, great Thom Hunter, my spiritual editor. And now for the special, humbling—make-me-cry—gratitude. To Jon and Laura, my son and daughter, for sharing their incredible wisdom and helping me figure out the way forward with their love. And to Douglas, my husband, without whom none of this—seriously—would be possible: not the life I lead now, nor the future we're creating together.

ABOUT THE AUTHOR

Robin Merle has been a senior executive for billion-dollar organizations. She is a veteran of the power, value, and identity wars at the top ranks. She has raised more than a half-billion dollars in philanthropy during her decades working with nonprofit organizations. She has served as a board member for three nonprofits in New York City, including the Association of Fundraising Professionals, New York City Chapter; the New York Women's Agenda; and Women In Development, New York (WID). She also has been a vice chair of National Philanthropy Day in New York. In 2017, she was named Woman of Achievement by WID for her leadership in fundraising and commitment to supporting women in the field. Robin is a frequent speaker at national conferences on fundraising and leadership.

Robin is proud to be a graduate of the first class of women at Rutgers College, earning a Bachelor of Arts. She has a Master of Arts from the Johns Hopkins University. Her short fiction has been published in various literary magazines. *Involuntary Exit* is her first nonfiction book. Robin divides her time between New York, Maine, and New Hampshire.

Author photo © Barry Morgenstein

SELECTED TITLES FROM SHE WRITES PRESS

She Writes Press is an independent publishing company founded to serve women writers everywhere. Visit us at www.shewritespress.com.

Falling Together: How to Find Balance, Joy, and Meaningful Change When Your Life Seems to be Falling Apart by Donna Cardillo. $16.95, 978-1-63152-077-8. A funny, big-hearted self-help memoir that tackles divorce, caregiving, burnout, major illness, fears, and low self-esteem—and explores the renewal that comes when we are able to meet these challenges with courage.

The Business of Being: Soul Purpose In and Out of the Workplace by Laurie Buchanan, PhD. $16.95, 978-1-63152-395-3. From a business plan and metrics to mission and goals with everything between—investors, clients and customers, marketing strategies, and goodwill development—this book clearly maps how to create personal transformation at the intersection of business and spirituality.

The Thriver's Edge: Seven Keys to Transform the Way You Live, Love, and Lead by Donna Stoneham. $16.95, 978-1-63152-980-1. A "coach in a book" from master executive coach and leadership expert Dr. Donna Stoneham, *The Thriver's Edge* outlines a practical road map to breaking free of the barriers keeping you from being everything you're capable of being.

This Way Up: Seven Tools for Unleashing Your Creative Self and Transforming Your Life by Patti Clark. $16.95, 978-1-63152-028-0. A story of healing for women who yearn to lead a fuller life, accompanied by a workbook designed to help readers work through personal challenges, discover new inspiration, and harness their creative power.

She Is Me: How Women Will Save the World by Lori Sokol, PhD. $16.95, 978-1-63152-715-9. Through interviews with women including Gloria Steinem, Billie Jean King, and Nobel Peace Prize recipient Leymah Gbowee, Sokol demonstrates how many of the traits thought to be typical of women—traits long considered to be soft and weak in our patriarchal culture—are actually proving more effective in transforming lives, securing our planet, and saving the world.